Arran Coastal Way

Jacquetta Megarry

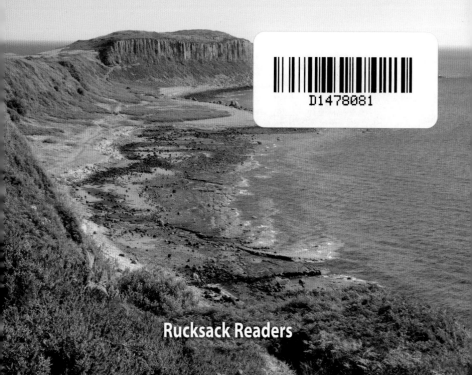

D1478081

Rucksack Readers

Arran Coastal Way

Second, fully revised edition published 2018 by Rucksack Readers, 6 Old Church Lane, Edinburgh, EH15 3PX, UK; first published 2008 in another format.

Phone   +44/0131 661 0262

Email: info@rucsacs.com

Website *www.rucsacs.com*

British Library cataloguing in publication data: a catalogue record for this book is available from the British Library.

ISBN 978-1-898481-79-9

Designed in Scotland by Ian Clydesdale (*www.workhorse.scot*)

Printed in Poland by Pario Print, Kraków on waterproof, biodegradable paper

Publisher's note

All information was checked prior to publication. However, changes are inevitable: take local advice and look out for waymarkers and other signage e.g. for diversions. Walkers are advised to check two websites for updates before setting out: *www.coastalway.co.uk* and *www.rucsacs.com/books/acw/*

Parts of the Way may be wet underfoot, others are remote, and the weather is unpredictable year-round. Boulder-fields require great care, especially in the wet, and a few parts of the Way are not safely passable around high tide. You are responsible for your own safety, for ensuring that your clothing, food and equipment are suited to your needs and that your intended walk can be safely completed in daylight. The publisher cannot accept any liability for any ill-health, injury or loss arising directly or indirectly from reading this book.

Feedback is welcome and will be rewarded

All feedback will be followed up, and readers whose comments lead to changes will be entitled to claim a free copy of our next edition upon publication. Please send emails to *info@rucsacs.com*.

Contents

Foreword

From the mainland, Arran is only a dozen miles across the Firth of Clyde, but on stepping ashore at Brodick pier, you feel as though you're entering an older, more peaceful world. The island has always held a special significance for me. It was while descending from the granite slabs of the A'Chir ridge some 45 years ago that I decided I wanted a job that would allow me to spend the rest of my life climbing mountains. The sun-kissed hills of Arran richly blessed me that day, as many times since.

Whilst Arran has always attracted climbers, some walkers are overawed by the steep, narrow ridges and soaring pinnacles of the island's northern mountains. Many would rather tackle something less dramatic, but still challenging enough to make an adventure. And so the Isle of Arran Coastal Way was conceived.

Arran's geology makes it ideal for coastal walking. The shallow coastal fringe of its raised beach encircles the island, and the Coastal Way follows it closely, seldom diverting inland. Whilst much of the route follows footpaths and stretches of beach, parts involve road-walking, albeit a very quiet and pleasant road, mostly on the west of the island. The Way has evolved and improved greatly over the years since I revisited Arran to open it in March 2003.

My own favourite section remains the toughest route option, from Kildonan to Whiting Bay past Dippin Head. No footpath tames this section, although all difficulties can be bypassed by heading inland from Kildonan on the main Way. With steep cliffs on one side and open sea on the other, there's something very satisfying in the uncompromising nature of the terrain. Rocky reefs run out towards the little lighthouse island of Pladda. This is rugged coastal walking at its finest.

Cameron McNeish

1 Planning and preparation

Best time of year

In theory, the Arran Coastal Way could be an all-year route because snow and ice are unlikely except on the high ground, even in winter. In practice, few would choose to walk it between November and March because of short hours of daylight, likely poor weather and limited accommodation.

In between, July/August tend to be busier months because of school holidays. The weather is apt to be drier in May/June, and September/October can be a good choice. The weather can be very changeable: be prepared for all four seasons in one day!

Gradient and terrain

The Way encircles the island in a 65-mile (105-km) loop that lies mainly at or near sea-level, with no serious altitude gains unless you opt for the shoulder or summit of Goat Fell: see page 38. In the first section, the main Way is low-level, barely breaking the 150 m contour on its way through Merkland Wood, and in poor weather this makes a better, as well as an easier, choice. However, on a fine day many will regard the panorama from the roof of Arran (874 m/2867 ft) as a highlight of their expedition.

The only other climb on the main Way is to about 200 m (660 ft) on the inland route from Kildonan to Whiting Bay. You might imagine that this makes it more strenuous than the coastal option – which stays at sea level and is 2 km shorter. Nothing could be further from the truth! Walking on Arran soon makes you realise that picking your way among boulders can be much more demanding – and slower going – than an extended climb on a firm surface, where you can get a rhythm going.

Across Brodick Bay to Goat Fell

The Way traverses a wide range of terrain, from tarmac road with grassy verge to tidal beaches with a mixture of boulders, shingle and sand. Rock-hopping across tidal beaches is not only slow, but also demands some agility and care, especially in the wet. The main Way goes over boulder-fields in two main places – An Scriodan (page 43) and around Bennan Head (page 59), with Dippin Head making an optional third (page 65). There is nothing to deter a walker of normal mobility, but allow yourself plenty of time and be sure to check the tide times: see below.

There are also some constructed paths, forest roads and hillside tracks where normal progress can be made. Depending on the recent weather and state of the tide, in places you'll have to take care to avoid wet feet. On tarmac, you may prefer trainers to boots, and on sandy beaches you may wish for crocs or bare feet.

 The percentage of road-walking is high in two sections, 3·4 and 3·5 (see Table 1), albeit along a scenic main road that carries fairly sparse traffic. Walk on the right-hand side so as to face oncoming traffic, and take to the verge or beach whenever suitable. Stay alert, especially near blind corners, and be prepared for the odd large vehicle.

South across Drumadoon Bay

Days, stages and duration

We recommend walking the Way anti-clockwise. When road-walking, this puts you next to the shore, making it easy to take to the beach where preferable, and giving unobstructed sea views. We describe the Way starting from Brodick because that's where the ferry arrives, but you can start anywhere, or indeed complete it in sections as day walks, or spread it over a couple of long weekends.

We present the walk in seven sections in Part 3; Table 1 shows the daily distances. Consider allowing more than seven days for your holiday. For example, you may want at least a day to see the sights of Brodick (see pages 31-33) or to visit the Holy Isle: see page 23. Or you may want to take a day off walking, especially if the weather is poor. Conversely, in great weather, you may want the chance to explore the mountainous interior.

However, if you've only a week to spare, you can shorten the walk by a day or two. Combining the first two sections makes for a very long day (17·6 mi/28·3 km), but is feasible for fit walkers who make an early start.

Table 1
Distances for the Way over seven sections

		miles	km	pages
	Brodick			
3·2		7·8	12·6	35-39
	Sannox			
3·3		9·8	15·7	40-45
	Lochranza			
3·4		8·9	14·3	46-50
	Imachar			
3·5		10·0	16·1	51-55
	Blackwaterfoot			
3·6		6·6	10·7	56-58
	Lagg			
3·7		11·3	18·3	59-66
	Whiting Bay			
3·8				67-73
	Brodick	10·9	17·5	
	Total	**65·3**	**105·2**	

Distances are measured along the route of the main Way: alternatives differ in length

You could save a further day by combining the third and fourth sections, going from Lochranza to Blackwaterfoot, perhaps using the bus or other transport to skip up to 10 miles (16 km) of road-walking between Catacol and the King's Cave car park. You could still include some splendid off-road walking by taking the Coire Lochan side-trip from Thundergay: see page 49. You might then use transport to Machrie, perhaps taking in the Standing Stones walk (page 18) and finish with the splendid King's Cave walk to Blackwaterfoot.

However, many people will find deep satisfaction in simply following the main Way to circumnavigate this beautiful island. A word of warning: when you are planning your trip, don't be misled by the modest distances in the table. Arran terrain makes for slow progress. Some off-road sections involve slow, tiring boulder-hopping, and in a couple of places there is no safe passage at high tide: see pages 10 and 59. Before deciding your schedule, think through some constraints on timing:

- hours of daylight
- tough terrain
- tide times
- (unless supported by a driver) the bus timetable.

Accommodation

Where you spend your overnights is another factor. Nowhere on Arran is much more than half an hour away from Brodick by car. In theory, if you plan carefully from the bus timetable, you could stay in Brodick or Whiting Bay for your entire holiday, using the bus to reach the start, and return from the finish, of each day's walk.

However, there's a choice of interesting hotels and B&Bs in many villages on the Way, and it would be a pity to miss staying in places such as Lochranza, Blackwaterfoot, Lagg, Kildonan and Lamlash. Budget options include bunkhouses, hostels and five campsites: see the table below.

A good compromise might be to spend a few nights each in two or three places, using the bus as needed, thus reducing the need to carry overnight stuff while walking. Since there's no accommodation at Imachar, after section 3·4 you would need to stay elsewhere, for example Lochranza, Pirnmill or Blackwaterfoot.

Table 2: Accommodation and facilities

	map page	B&B/hotel	hostel / bunkhouse *	campsite *	pub/café	food shop, carryout
Brodick	37	✓	✓	within ✓1½ miles	✓	✓
Corrie	37	✓			✓	
Sannox	37	✓			✓	
Lochranza	42	✓	✓	✓	✓	
Catacol	47	✓				
Pirnmill	47	✓			✓	✓
Machrie	53				✓	
Blackwaterfoot	57	✓		within ✓2 miles		✓
Lagg	60	✓			✓*	
Kilmory	60		✓			
Kildonan	61	✓		✓		
Whiting Bay	63	✓			✓	✓
Lamlash	69	✓		within ✓1 mile	✓	✓

* may be open in season only: check for exact dates

Many walkers prefer to have the whole trip organised for them as a package, and some independent walkers want their overnight baggage transferred; for details of service providers, see page 74. As of 2017, at least 10 companies offered a range of services.

Finally, if you intend to camp, be aware that there are campsites at only five places on the Way: Glen Rosa (near Brodick), Lochranza, Bridgend/Shiskine (2 miles/3·6 km from Blackwaterfoot),

Auchrannie House

Kildonan and Middleton's, near Lamlash. All are marked on our map. In addition, under the *Scottish Outdoor Access Code*, wild camping is allowed for a couple of nights anywhere that access rights apply, but various responsibilities accompany that right. See the panel on page 11 for more about the *Code*.

Waymarking

Major improvements have been made to waymarking since the route opened in 2003, but a number of options have been added, so there are many more junctions and you still need to be vigilant. All recent waymarking carries the gannet logo, although there may still be places on beaches where a splash of paint provides your reassurance. Be aware that where the route splits, the alternative route is marked with a red disc, whereas the main route is marked with yellow discs.

Carry a compass and try to stay aware of where you are on our mapping at all times. You may wish to carry also the OS Explorer map, but as of 2017 the route was not marked on it: see page 75.

Mostly if you keep the sea on your right you are unlikely to become seriously lost, but your walk will be needlessly tiring or frustrating if you stray off-route. There is also a safety issue: knowing that there's a main road on the cliff-top to your left is of little use if you don't know where the escape route is and you've unwisely ignored the rising tide and/or failing light!

Be aware that the tidal nature of Arran's coast means that in places there is no single best path. At low tide you may have an easier walk on firm sand or shingle, whereas at high tide you may be forced higher, to scramble over large boulders or amongst overgrown vegetation. This is all part of the Way's distinctive character: excessive reliance on waymarking won't work on Arran.

Tide awareness

Once on the island, you can find tide times from local newspapers, hotels, bars and the iCentre at Brodick ferry terminal. A handy booklet is published annually with tide data for many places around the island: in 2017 it cost £1.50. If you have access only to Brodick Bay tide times, allow for time differences of up to 25 minutes. Tide tables may give times in GMT; if so, add one hour when British Summer Time is in force. For online tidal information in advance, and dates for BST see page 74.

There are two high tides daily, about 12½ hours apart, with two low tides in between. Roughly speaking, the high tides tomorrow will happen nearly an hour later than those of today, and so on, day after day.

High tides are higher, and low tides lower, shortly after full and new moon, especially around the spring and autumn equinoxes. Weather, wind and waves also affect how dangerous places such as Bennan Head or Dippin Head could be around high tide. If in doubt, don't push your luck: use an escape route and never advance into danger on a rising tide.

The Scottish Outdoor Access Code

Everyone has the right to be on most land and inland water providing they act responsibly. Your access rights and responsibilities are explained fully in the Scottish Outdoor Access Code.

Whether you're in the outdoors or managing the outdoors, the key things are to
- **take responsibility for your own actions**
- **respect the interests of other people**
- **care for the environment.**

Find out more by visiting
www.outdooraccess-scotland.com or
by contacting Scottish Natural Heritage;
see page 74 for details.

The *Scottish Outdoor Access Code* interprets access rights established by law. The Arran Coastal Way passes through countryside which provides a livelihood for its residents. It is your responsibility to show consideration for them and their livestock.

Lambing takes places between March and June: never disturb ewes or cattle which are, or may be pregnant, nor approach young lambs or calves. Cattle can be fiercely protective of their young: give them a wide berth, and keep watching how they react to your presence.

Dogs

Responsible owners are entitled to take their dogs along the Way. However, think carefully before deciding to bring your pet. Dogs must be kept under close control, not only to avoid stress to livestock and wildlife, but also for their own safety. Never allow your dog to approach livestock that are, or may be, pregnant, let alone if they are with young. If you are walking with your dog on the lead, keep well away from cattle: both dog and owner are endangered by this combination. Stay alert to the animals' body language, and if cattle react aggressively to you, let any dog off the lead, stay calm and escape the field by the shortest, safest route.

Before deciding to take your dog along the Way, consider these points:

1 Some sections of the Way have stiles that you will have to lift your dog over. This can be strenuous and/or awkward, depending on the dog's weight and attitude.
2 Many accommodations do not accept dogs (except assistance dogs): check carefully before booking.
3 You must clean up after your dog if it fouls the footpath.
4 Dogs may disturb ground-nesting birds or young mammals: shore-nesting birds are very vulnerable, so keep your dog under extra-close control during the breeding season (April to July).

Your rights and responsibilities when walking with a dog are listed in the leaflet *Dog Owners* from Scottish Natural Heritage: see page 74.

Travel planning

Most people arrive on Arran after a ferry crossing of 13 miles (21 km) to Brodick from Ardrossan: see Table 3 for distances. Even if you drive to the ferry, you don't need to take your car over if your main goal is to walk the Way. There's secure car parking at Ardrossan and a bus service on the island: see page 13. If you must take a car, however, advance booking is essential. There are at least 4 or 5 ferries daily (and up to 10 in high season), journey time 55 minutes with a minimum check-in time of 30 minutes for vehicles, 10 minutes for pedestrians. Reduced ferry fares for vehicles since 2016 have made Arran's roads very busy in summer months, especially in the eastern part of the island.

A smaller ferry plies between Lochranza and Kintyre, calling at Claonaig in summer and Tarbert in winter; vehicles must be booked in winter. Note that timetables change twice a year, usually in late October and March. For fares, timetables and bookings for all ferries, contact CalMac: *www.calmac.co.uk*.

Trains from the south and west arrive at Glasgow Central, from which trains take about an hour to reach Ardrossan. From north and east Scotland trains arrive at Glasgow Queen Street, with a short transfer to Central. Boat trains normally connect with the ferry. Stay on until Ardrossan Harbour, the end of the line.

If arriving by air at Glasgow airport, take the bus to Paisley Gilmour Street station in time to join the boat train as above. From Prestwick Airport, take a train to Kilwinning station, then change for Ardrossan. There are about 4 trains daily.

Table 3		
Distances to Ardrossan from various places		
	miles	*km*
Ayr	20	32
Edinburgh	80	129
Glasgow (city centre)	35	56
Glasgow Airport (Paisley)	27	43
Prestwick Airport	16	26

Bus and ferry routes

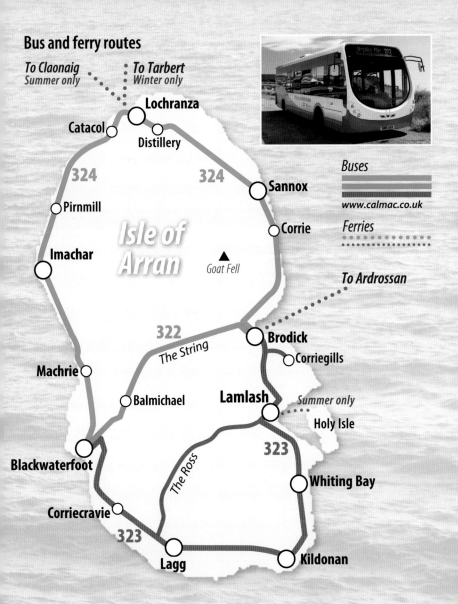

To Claonaig
Summer only

To Tarbert
Winter only

Lochranza

Catacol

Distillery

324

324

Sannox

Pirnmill

Corrie

Isle of Arran

▲ Goat Fell

Imachar

To Ardrossan

322

The String

Brodick

Machrie

Corriegills

Balmichael

Lamlash

Summer only

Blackwaterfoot

Holy Isle

323

The Ross

Whiting Bay

Corriecravie

323

Lagg

Kildonan

Buses

www.calmac.co.uk

Ferries

Arran is well served by its bus service and coastal road. Although there are only about 4 or 5 buses a day, the service is reliable, and timed to connect with most ferries and other buses. For example, the String/South Island service waits for the regular ferries, and if you change at Blackwaterfoot you can connect with the String/North Island service.

To ride right around the island, use the Arran Rural Rover (unlimited bus travel for the day). The bus station is at Brodick Pier. Obtain the free *Area Transport Guide* leaflet for details: it's available on the ferry and at the VisitScotland iCentre in Brodick.

Fitness and preparation

If you haven't done much walking before, it's advisable to tackle the Way with someone who is experienced, especially in the use of map and compass. Well before you leave for Arran, do a few all-day walks to test your footwear and to build up fitness. If you are carrying for yourself, practise carrying a loaded rucksack.

The Arran Coastal Way is difficult to compare with other long-distance routes. Taken slowly, avoiding the hardest boulder-fields and staying low-level from Brodick to Sannox, it is less demanding than, say, the West Highland Way. However, many walkers who complete the Way within 5 or 6 days, including all boulder-fields and summiting Goat Fell, find it much *more* challenging. Don't underestimate this walk. It may not be the ideal choice for your first long-distance walk, especially if you plan to walk alone. For advice on choosing and buying gear, obtain our *Notes for novices*: see page 75.

Packing checklist

This list separates essential and desirable items. If you haven't worn your waterproof trousers recently, test them before you go, while there's still time to re-proof, mend or replace them. Gaiters are great for keeping boots and feet dry and mud-free, and for protection from brambles, nettles and bracken where ticks may lurk. Protection from the sun is also important: take both hat and sunscreen. Walking poles will be useful only if you already like them, and in places may be a liability, e.g. when crossing boulder-fields. It helps to have rucksack loops that let you stow the poles while scrambling.

If you are camping, you will need much more gear (tent, sleeping bag and mat, food and cooking kit) and a much larger rucksack in which to carry everything. If wild camping, remember that safe drinking water needs to be boiled or purified. Using a baggage-handling service may be a better option unless you are experienced.

Essential
- rucksack with waterproof cover or liner(s)
- comfortable, waterproof walking boots
- specialist walking socks
- waterproof jacket and over-trousers
- clothing in layers (tops, trousers, jacket)
- hat (for warmth and/or sun protection)
- gloves
- guidebook, maps and compass
- whistle and torch (for emergencies)
- water carrier and plenty of water (or purification tablets)
- enough food to last between supply points
- first aid kit, including blister treatment
- toilet tissue (preferably biodegradable)
- personal toiletries
- insect repellent and sun protection
- cash and credit cards; 3 free cash machines in Brodick, but getting cash elsewhere can be difficult or expensive.

Desirable
- walking pole(s)
- gaiters
- trainers and perhaps also crocs
- spare dry socks to change into
- camera with spare batteries and memory cards
- binoculars – useful for watching wildlife
- notebook and pen
- pouch or secure pockets for keeping small items handy *and safe*
- mobile phone and charger.

> **Mobile phone reception is very patchy in Arran. Never rely on one for personal safety. In 2017, the network with best coverage was Vodafone.**

2·1 Scotland in miniature

Arran is Scotland's most southerly inhabited island, and its seventh largest, about 19 miles (30 km) long by up to 10 miles (16 km) wide. Its position in the Firth of Clyde makes it very accessible, a mere 13 miles from the mainland, just over two hours from the heart of Glasgow.

The moniker *Scotland in miniature* has some validity. Like mainland Scotland, it is divided by the Highland Boundary Fault, with rugged mountains in the north, and fertile, low-lying land in the south. It has a cross-section of Scotland's habitats, and a wide range of its wildlife. Unlike Scotland as a whole, however, its population lives in coastal villages linked by the main road, and the island's interior is virtually uninhabited.

The number of Arranachs has fluctuated over time, with a peak of about 6500 in 1823, followed by progressive decline that has been checked in recent years. The present official figure is about 5000 residents, well over half of whom live in the three eastern villages: in order of size, these are Lamlash, Brodick and Whiting Bay. Tourism. Tourism is the main source of employment, and resident numbers are swollen by thousands of summer visitors.

The prevailing wind is south-westerly, and the climate moist and temperate. Mild winters allow palm trees and sub-tropical plants to flourish. Rainfall is high, especially in the east: Brodick gets about 89 in (225 cm) of rain per annum, compared to Arran's west coast at 70 in (170 cm) – and Glasgow's 35 in (90 cm). However, May and June tend to be drier months, and many of the photographs in this book were taken during a single memorable visit one October.

Most of the island has very noticeable raised beaches. After the last Ice Age, there was a massive release of weight when the ice melted. The land rose, creating raised beaches with former sea caves. In fact, there are two raised beach levels: the older 100-ft (30 m) one, and the newer (10,000 years old) at only 25 feet above sea level.

Raised beaches provide the perfect platform for the main road which encircles the island and is 56 miles (90 km) long. Together with two strategic roads across it, The String and The Ross, Arran is wonderfully easy to get around.

Arran's mountainous north, seen from Kintyre

Geology

Arran is the classic destination for field geology. Its rich variety of rock formations is unrivalled in the British Isles, perhaps in Europe. Students of geology come to Arran from all over the world to do their fieldwork.

Huge rock near the Black Cave

As you follow the Way, you can't fail to notice the remarkable variety of colours, shapes and formations in the rocks – colossal roadside boulders on the Corrie/Sannox shore, spectacular rock falls north of Sannox, dramatic caves and cliffs near Drumadoon Point, and impressive dark rocks around the Black Cave.

Scattered along the south coast are dykes of igneous rocks – thin fingers pointing out to sea. These relatively young rocks (about 60 million years old) have been left standing proud after weathering has ground down the older, softer Triassic rocks that surrounded them. Around Lochranza are the Cambrian schists, extremely old at about 550 million years. Schist is a metamorphic rock – in simple terms, ancient sands and muds that (over a long period) have been turned into hard rock by extreme pressure and temperature.

Arran played a pivotal role in the thinking of James Hutton (1726-97), the father of modern geology. Hutton visited Arran in 1787, searching for igneous rocks. He had already published his *Theory of the Earth* suggesting continuing tension between two processes, weathering down the mountains and upthrust by volcanic events, over long periods of time.

In 1645 Archbishop Ussher had calculated (from the Bible) that the earth began on 23 October 4004 BC, and Hutton grew up in an era when this Biblical timescale was accepted. On a walk near Newton Point, however, he noticed a strange angular rock formation. The photograph shows what became known as his Unconformity: the very old rocks in the foreground (Cambrian schist) slope inland, whilst the younger sandstones above them dip towards the sea. They are lying unconformably on the older rocks, with a layer of soil between the two.

Basalt dyke, with Ailsa Craig in stormy background

Hutton's Angular Unconformity

Since sedimentary rocks are deposited in horizontal layers, it takes eons for geological processes (such as heat, pressure and folding) to force them up at an angle, and longer still for erosion to wear them down. Between the two kinds of rock at different angles, Hutton realised that the time-gap must have been millions, not thousands, of years. He established the non-Biblical, and highly controversial, concept of deep time.

The gap between those two layers is now thought to be about 100 million years, which is far greater than Hutton realised. But this and other Unconformities proved his theory that the earth was unimaginably older than anybody had thought. Much criticised in his lifetime, his radical ideas had a massive impact, not only then but also, 50 years later, on the young Charles Darwin. Hutton had looked into the abyss of time, and found 'no vestige of a beginning and no prospect of an end'. Without him, Darwin's theory of natural selection would have been unthinkable.

Sea caves north of Drumadoon Point

2·2 Pre-history and history

The Stone Age farmers left many traces in hut circles, burial cairns and stone circles. Many standing stones – tall monoliths – are scattered around the island. The Way passes by ancient chambered cairns at Torrylin and the Giants' Graves: see pages 60 and 62.

Many forts or duns stand in prominent sites atop hills, dating from the Iron Age about 2000 - 2500 years ago. They were stone structures used for defence or residence, or perhaps both. Their shape is usually a distinctive oval mound, grass-covered, sometimes with stones visible. The Way passes several such forts, the impressive Doon Fort, the fort near Glenashdale and Dun Fionn: see pages 54, 70 and 72.

Machrie Moor contains one of the finest range of ancient monuments in Scotland. Most prominent are six Bronze Age stone circles, about 3800-4000 years old and made of red sandstone or granite. Two of them stand on the sites of Neolithic timber circles which are 500 years older still. The moor also has scattered hut circles, chambered cairns and monoliths. The tallest of the monoliths is 18 feet/ 5·5 m high. The interpretation board helps to visualise what's missing where other stones have fallen.

> *i*
>
> **Machrie Moor Stone Circles walk**
>
> Leave the main road 250 m south of Machrie Water at the stile signposted 'Machrie Moor Stone Circle 1 mile': see page 51. Follow the track south-east across the fields, making a dogleg and passing the Moss Farm Road Stone Circle. Climbing slightly, you'll notice stones and cairns scattered over the moorland, once home to a settled agricultural community. It's actually 2 km from the A841 that you finally reach the stile to the main site with its Historic Scotland interpretation board. Allow an hour for the round trip, more if you want time to wander about this atmospheric site.

By about 500 AD, Gaelic-speaking settlers from Northern Ireland, known as the Scotti, had extended their kingdom of Dalriada to south-west Scotland including Arran. They brought their Gaelic language, still spoken on Arran (by dwindling numbers) until the 20th century. In the 6th century, Irish missionary saints such as Brendan, Columba, Molaise and Donan brought Christianity.

Standing stones, Machrie Moor

From about 800 AD Arran fell under Viking rule, and its Viking legacy is obvious in many place names. In 1263, the Scots defeated the Vikings under King Haakon at the Battle of Largs, ending the era of Viking domination.

By 1371, Robert II (a Stewart successor to Robert the Bruce) had become King of Scots, and used Arran as his hunting ground while based at Brodick Castle: see page 33 Later centuries saw violent fighting between various feudal lords. The Way passes the impressive ruins of castles at Lochranza and (coastal option) Kildonan: see pages 45 and 65 .

The Hamilton family's link with Arran dates from 1503 when James, Lord Hamilton married Mary Stewart, daughter of James II of Scotland. Their son James was created Earl of Arran, and Brodick Castle and most of Arran belonged to the family for centuries afterwards.

Major changes in agricultural practice led to the Arran Clearances of the early 19th century. Communal 'runrig' farms were abolished, more profitable sheep and deer introduced, and hapless tenants cleared ruthlessly, often by burning their homes. Some left for jobs in industrial towns, others for the New World, especially Canada. Migration was encouraged, with half the fare paid by the 10th Duke of Hamilton. There's a memorial to the 1829 voyage to Quebec City by 86 emigrants: see below.

In the late 19th century, Arran started to be seen as a holiday destination. Later, in the heyday of the Clyde steamers, visitors would rent a house for a summer month, and Arranachs would move into back quarters for the letting season. The steamers barely carried cars at first, but increasing demand led to frequent rollon-rolloff ferries and a trend for visitors to stay for shorter periods. The appeal of outdoor activities from golf to geology is still very strong, and many overseas visitors, especially from Canada, come to Arran to trace their families.

Arran Clearances Memorial, Lamlash

2·3 Scotch whisky and Arran

Whisky is made from just three natural ingredients: grain, yeast and water. A sequence of processes – malting, milling, mashing, fermenting and distilling – turns the grain into a strong colourless spirit, which is stored in oak barrels or casks before being bottled and sold as a precious amber fluid. Although a small amount of specialised whisky is bottled at cask strength (50-60% alcohol), most is mixed with water to reduce the alcohol level to about 40%.

By law, the label 'Scotch whisky' can be applied only if it has been wholly distilled and matured in Scotland, and has spent at least three years in the cask. There are two kinds of Scotch: malt and grain. Malt whisky is made only from malted barley, and is distilled in batches in a traditional copper pot still. By contrast, grain whisky may contain unmalted barley and other cereals, and is created in a patent still in a continuous, mechanised process. This section is about malt whisky.

'Single malt' means whisky that is 100% pure and from a single distillery, as opposed to blended whisky. Well-known brands are blends of grain and malt whiskies, with small amounts of many malts contributing up to 50%. The proportions of ingredients in each blend 'recipe' are a closely guarded secret.

Malt whisky is to grain as chateau-bottled wine is to table wine: it has more bouquet, has been matured for longer and is more expensive, sometimes much more so. Experts can identify a whisky uniquely just by 'nosing' it. The diagram opposite shows the sequence from malting to maturing.

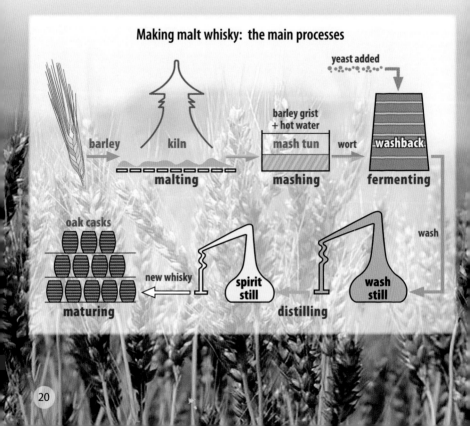

Making malt whisky: the main processes

yeast added

barley   kiln   barley grist + hot water   mash tun   wort   washback

malting   **mashing**   **fermenting**

oak casks   new whisky   spirit still   wash still   wash

maturing   **distilling**

'Malting' is the process of making the barley 'sprout' (germinate) by soaking, turning, heating and drying in kilns fuelled with peat. This breaks down starches and helps to convert them into sugars. Traditionally, each distillery had its own malting house (with a distinctive chimney) but nowadays most obtain malted barley from central sources.

The dried malt is first ground or milled to make a coarse flour or grist. Then it goes for mashing in a large cylinder (the mash tun), where it's mixed with hot water and stirred to dissolve the sugars produced during malting. This produces a sugary liquid or wort, which is drawn off for fermenting, whilst the residue or draff is converted into dark pellets for cattle feed.

Fermentation takes place in large tanks called washbacks, where yeast is added and, under close temperature control, the sugar converted into crude alcohol. The process takes about 48 hours and the fermented liquid is called wash – a kind of sweet barley beer with about 5-7% alcohol by volume.

Distillation is the final stage before storage and bottling, and it takes place in pot stills. The wash is heated carefully so that most of the alcohol is vapourised whilst the water is left behind: alcohol has a lower boiling point (78°C) than water (100°C). The alcohol vapour rises up the wash still and passes along its swan neck to be condensed and collected in a water-cooled coil or worm.

The first distillation creates low wines, a portion of which is distilled again in a second, smaller spirit still to create high wines or new whisky. (The first and last portions of the batch are recycled into the wash still, and only the 'heart' of the run goes to the spirit still.) The whole process is controlled by a stillman using a spirit safe – a glass-fronted box through which the sprit passes after it comes off the still. (The box is kept locked by Customs and Excise: duty is not paid on whisky until it is bottled and sold.)

Water may be added to reduce the strength of the new whisky to 63·5%, the ideal strength for maturing it. Storage is in oak casks used previously for sherry or (more commonly) bourbon. Since oak is permeable, harsh elements of the new spirit escape and air and moisture get in. Throughout storage, there is a loss of volume and of alcoholic strength known as the 'angel's share' – up to 2% per annum. For malt whiskies which are typically matured for 8 years or longer, this adds considerably to costs.

Stripped of its mystique and jargon, the process is essentially simple: malting, mashing, fermenting, distilling and maturing. However, every detail at each stage matters: the water source, the peat used in malting, the exact temperature and duration of the mashing, the precise shape and height of the pot still, as well as the time, temperature and proportions taken at each stage of distillation, the previous history of the casks and the microclimate during storage. Above all, the soft air and spring or burn water are considered vitally important to the final flavour. This may explain why nobody has succeeded in making anything that resembles Scottish whisky outside of Scotland, although many have tried.

Whisky-making on Arran

The art of whisky-making reached Scotland from Ireland in the 16th century, and gradually spread to places with suitable resources. During the 17th and 18th century, private stills were commonplace around Arran. In 1781, the Government outlawed private distilling and introduced punitive taxation, enforced by unpopular excisemen. Illicit stills persisted in Arran's secluded hills and glens, some surviving well into the 20th century. After a drastic reduction in duty in 1823, legal distilling became worthwhile, but Arran's last official distillery at Lagg stopped production in 1837.

The creation of the new distillery in Lochranza in 1995 was the work of the late Harold Currie (1924-2016) who worked closely with its architect David Hutchison. Currie set up the Isle of Arran Distillers Ltd, insistent that all aspects of production should be traditional, with copper stills and wooden washbacks. The site was chosen for its natural water source: from Loch na Davie, water drops 360 m/1200 feet through the glen to the distillery 'cleansed by granite and softened by peat'.

At its royal opening, a good omen was the flypast by a pair of golden eagles nesting in the nearby glen. Since then, the distillery has widened its range of whiskies and increased production. In 2017 the two original stills were replaced by four new ones, and work began on a new distillery at Lagg, to be dedicated to making heavily peated malt whisky. When both distilleries are working, their combined capacity will be up to 165,000 litres of spirit per year.

> **Isle of Arran Distillery**
> The distillery lies only 600 m south-east of the Way, and worth visiting for its exhibition and Casks café. In season (early March to late October) the Visitor Centre is open daily from 10.00 to 17.30. Out of season, check opening times: visit www.arranwhisky.com or phone 01770 830 264. Tours leave on the hour (normally 10.00 to 16.00), and include a short video and tastings; in 2017 the cost was £8. Booking is advised: bookings@arranwhisky.com.

Pot stills, Isle of Arran Distillery

2·4 The Holy Isle

Holy Isle is the shapely island that shelters Lamlash Bay. It's only about 2 miles long by half a mile wide (3 km by 1 km), but offers a great walk with rugged scenery and impressive views from its rocky summit, Mullach Mor (314 m/1030 ft).

The island is also home to an interesting collection of animal rare breeds, and has an important religious past, dating from the 6th century when Celtic Saint Molaise lived here as a hermit. There is historic evidence of a later Christian monastery and burial ground at its north-west end, though no traces remain.

In 1992, it was acquired by the Rokpa Trust, Tibetan Buddhists who run a variety of courses, retreats and environmental projects. Although the eastern half of the island is closed, visitors are welcome to complete a scenic circular walk: see page below. Please keep to the well-signed footpath and respect the rules. The free leaflet explains the various requests: don't bring pets, alcohol or drugs, but do bring refreshments.

In season, the ferry plies frequently from Lamlash: see panel. The boat lands at the converted farmhouse which opened as the Centre for World Peace and Health in 2004. Although it's feasible to walk the circuit inside three hours or so, a more relaxed visit takes longer. Either way, it would be a pity to leave Arran without visiting its miniature cousin.

You can normally buy refreshments and can even arrange to stay at the Centre: visit **www.holyisle. org** or phone 01770 601 100. The book *Holy Island* gives detail on its history, wildlife and the Buddhist project: see page 75.

> **By ferry to the Holy Isle**
> *The ferry season is usually Easter to October, when (subject to weather and tides) the boat leaves from the Old Pier, Lamlash up to 3 times a day. The crossing takes about ten minutes and bookings don't apply (except for groups): just turn up. Be sure to confirm your return plans with the skipper on your outward trip. Out of season, phone to find out if and when the boat will go. In 2017 the adult return fare was £12. Phone 01770 700 463 or 07970 771 960.*

The walk

This circuit is described from the boat jetty clockwise, outward by the hilly spine, returning by the easy walk up the western coast. There are polite signs to guide you, and the path is well-defined, but walking boots are required. During or after wet weather, care is needed, especially on the steep descent at the southern end.

Stupas lead to the Centre for World Peace and Health, Holy Isle

Eriskay ponies running free on Holy Isle

You may meet the rare breeds that run free and coexist peacefully. Hardy Eriskay ponies are descended from four animals introduced in 1981. The small brown horned animals are Soay sheep, a rare breed from the Outer Hebrides. They probably date from the Bronze Age, but were introduced to Holy Isle in 1970. The white, long-horned Saanen goats are more native, having lived here for seven centuries.

Start your walk from the jetty, heading east uphill at the north side of the Centre. The path soon veers south-east, climbing the spine of the island to the cairn at Mullach Beag (246 m/800 ft). There are good views from here, but there's better in store.

The path descends south-east into the saddle, then climbs, steeply in places, to Mullach Mor. The trig point is decked with prayer flags and coins as

Summit of Mullach Mor (314 m/1030 ft)

offerings, and can be a great place to picnic in good weather. Its modest height belies its splendid unobstructed views over Arran, the Firth of Clyde with Ailsa Craig, and the Ayrshire coast.

The descent is steep in parts, but not protracted, and at its foot you have a choice. Turn left for a short diversion to Pillar Rock Lighthouse, or turn right to continue the circuit, soon passing the lighthouse cottages (used for the traditional Buddhist retreat of three years and three months).

Pillar Rock lighthouse

St Molaise's Cave (inset: wall painting)

Turn right (north) in front of the retreat, to follow the coastal path which soon passes rocks painted with Buddhist images. Soon after the last of these, a small wooden bench heralds St Molaise's Cave, just off to your right. Molaise (566-640 AD) was only 20 years old when he became a hermit here, later being ordained in Rome and then returning to Ireland. Centuries later, in 1263 the Vikings visited Holy Isle and Vigleikr cut runes with his name on the cave wall.

Just before the cave is the holy spring, known as the Healing Well, which looks more like a clear, rocky pool. There's a metal ladle for those who wish to sample its 'healing properties'. Between here and the cave is a huge level-topped block of stone, known as the Judgement Stone or St Molaise's Table, possibly used for preaching or announcing judgements. From the cave, it's only a mile (1·6 km) of flat walking back to the jetty and the Centre.

Green Tara, Mother of all the Buddhas, rock painting

Summit cairn on Mullach Beag

2·5 Habitats and wildlife

Arran's mild climate and mixed scenery makes it home to a huge variety of plants and animals. Much of the island is recognised as a Site of Special Scientific Interest. With few predators and limited threat from human settlement, the animals are surprisingly approachable. In the space of a few days one October, I saw every creature photographed in this section, in most cases from nearby and in broad daylight.

Red-breasted mergansers

As ever, however, animals and birds are more active in the early morning and late evening, so these are the best times to seek them, if possible carrying binoculars and moving quietly. An interesting feature of the island is the complete absence of certain species that are commonplace on the mainland. You won't see any magpies, nor moles, foxes nor, mercifully, any grey squirrels: see page 29 for its charming red cousin.

The Way passes through three main habitats – coastal, woodland and upland – of which the first is clearly dominant.

Coastal

Much of the Way runs along or just above the beach. Arran has over 900 species of flowering plants, mainly on the raised beaches and in the hedgerows. You will see gardens shrubs such as fuchsia and buddleia flourishing in the wild. At any time of year, even in December, Arran is in flower.

Around the coastline, you'll see lots of ducks, including red-breasted mergansers and eider ducks. You are certain to see seals, both common and Atlantic grey, especially along the Corrie/Sannox shore, near Lochranza and also in the south, near Kildonan. Around low tide they cluster in larger groups; when the tide is in, lone seals bask on isolated rocks.

The common seal is smaller than the grey, and not as long-lived (20-30 years, compared with 35 or more years for grey). Distinguishing them is easy if you're close enough to see their heads: the grey has a flat top to its head, whereas the common seal has a rounded forehead and V-shaped nostrils. From a distance, the common seal is smaller and sleeker, often arching its body; the grey looks more lumpish ashore.

Grey seal (female)

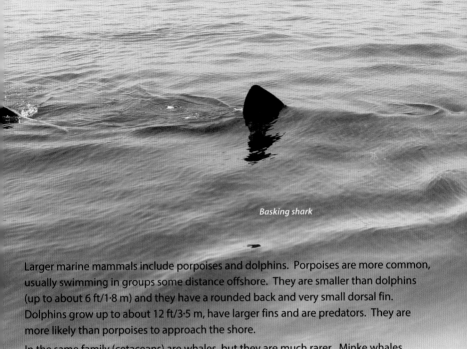

Basking shark

Larger marine mammals include porpoises and dolphins. Porpoises are more common, usually swimming in groups some distance offshore. They are smaller than dolphins (up to about 6 ft/1·8 m) and they have a rounded back and very small dorsal fin. Dolphins grow up to about 12 ft/3·5 m, have larger fins and are predators. They are more likely than porpoises to approach the shore.

In the same family (cetaceans) are whales, but they are much rarer. Minke whales, which grow up to 36 ft/11 m in length, occasionally visit Arran. Your best chance of seeing any of these marine mammals is in very calm weather, using binoculars.

Between August and October, you may be lucky enough to spot the large black fin of a basking shark: see above. These huge fish (up to 36ft/11 m) feed on nothing but plankton, and have no teeth. They are second in size only to whale sharks, and internationally recognised as an endangered species: see page 74 for the website.

Arran has a good number of otters around its coast, but you need luck and patience to see this shy mammal. On land, an otter look similar to a mink, but much larger, with a broad tapering tail. In the water, they leave a V-shaped wake when swimming. Your best chance is around dawn or dusk on a quiet section of coast. The otter in the photograph below is feeding on codling.

There's a wide range of sea birds, including gulls, fulmar and gannet. The gannet is easily recognised by its amazing aerobatics: they glide low over the water, hunting, then climb very high, folding their wings to dive-bomb their prey at speeds of over 80 kph (50 mph).

Gannet

If you see large black birds standing on rocks with their wings outstretched or diving for fish, they are probably shag or cormorant. Shag are smaller and more common here; cormorant are distinguished by a heavier bill and white throat patch.

The oystercatcher is a striking bird with a long orange bill and, in flight, an obvious M-shape in white-on-black. Unlike inland Scotland, where they are summer visitors, in Arran you'll see them year-round, sometimes in large flocks on the beaches. When disturbed, their piercing shrieks are unmistakeable.

A very different, crooning 'ah-ooo' sound is made by the eider duck, one of the world's largest and longest-living sea ducks. Drakes have the striking black and white breeding plumage shown in the photograph. Females are dull brown and mottled, well camouflaged for sitting on their nests, where they pluck down from their breasts for lining. In Iceland, this is still harvested for luxury duvets, jackets and eiderdowns.

Woodland

On the first day, the Way passes through a fine stretch of mixed woodland in Brodick Country Park en route for Merkland Wood. There are mature spreading oak and beech, mixed with slender birch, ash and rowan. Conifers include Scots pine, the only pine tree native to Britain, with a sprinkling of imported species such as Sitka and Norway spruce. In spring, the colours in the Country Park's famous collection of rhododendrons are spectacular. In autumn, foliage and berries show their warm colours.

Mature beech in autumn

28

North of Sannox, and between Lochranza and Catacol, the Way passes through patches of mixed natural woodland. In spring, wild flowers flourish here, with patches of bluebells (wild hyacinth) and red campion. Wild primrose grows in clumps, with yellow flowers and crinkly bright green leaves.

Between Whiting Bay and Lamlash, the main Way runs through native woodland, partly on boardwalk, with superb displays of wildflowers *Arran whitebeam*
in spring. Glen Catacol is home to the endemic Arran whitebeam (Sorbus arranensis). To visit these endangered trees, just before you cross the Abhainn Mor make a 50-m detour inland to their enclosure: see page 49 bullet 3.

Arran is one of the last strongholds of the agile red squirrel, elsewhere threatened by disease and competition from its non-native grey cousin. They're quite easy to spot, especially in autumn when hoarding food for the winter. If you see stripped pine cones on the ground, they've almost certainly been chewed by red squirrels. They occur anywhere on the island, especially in Brodick Country Park, the grounds of Auchrannie and even on garden bird feeders.

Upland

The Way climbs significantly in only two places: the main Way reaches 200 m above sea level in the woodland north of Kildonan, and the Goat Fell option climbs to 630 m/2050 ft (at the shoulder). Ground cover is rough grass, with blaeberry (bilberry) and heather, in places also with bog myrtle. These provide important habitat for brown hare and grouse. Tall heather is important also for the hen harrier, which preys on small mammals and birds. Arran has 5% of the UK's breeding population of this beautiful raptor.

Gorse (or whin) grows in dense, spiny patches with yellow almond-scented flowers almost year-round. Thorny brambles (blackberry) flourish, providing a heavy crop of fruit in autumn. Lower slopes have huge areas of bracken, the commonest and most invasive of ferns, but Arran has over 45 other species of fern.

Red squirrel on birch branch

Golden eagle

Higher up, the vegetation becomes sparser, but still supports small mammals such as vole, mice, rabbits and hare. The latter two are important food for the golden eagle. Eagles also take carrion, on Arran mainly dead lambs or young red deer.

Eagle sightings are normally rare, and from afar. Visitors often mistake the more common buzzard for eagle. The eagle has a huge wing-span of about 2 m, double that of a buzzard. From a distance, the eagle looks a bit like a flying plank, whereas buzzards have a rounder wing shape and may be seen hovering and soaring, and perhaps heard mewing. A pair of eagles live above Lochranza, and the mountainous interior of the north island offers your best chance of a sighting.

If the eagle is the iconic bird of the Scottish Highlands, then the red deer is its iconic mammal. On Arran, they are commonplace, mostly kept in the northern half by a deer fence right across the island. In October, you will hear the loud bellow of the stags in rut, each one trying to collect a group of hinds and fighting off other stags with clashing antlers.

Red deer are easy to spot around Lochranza, especially out of season where they invade unprotected gardens, stroll on the golf course and even wade around the beach. On the mainland, they are normally seen only from a distance on the skyline. On Arran, they stay upland in summer, feeding on the sweet grasses, but in winter they descend for heather and other foliage. Culling is essential, to control numbers and to prevent the destruction of habitat which would lead to slow death by starvation.

Red deer hinds grazing on Lochranza golf course

Brodick Country Park

Castle main gate

Brodick Bay

Arran Coastal Way

Brodick Castle

Footpath

A841

Cladach

Mountain Rescue Post

Fisherman's Walk

Duchess Court

North Beach

Glenrosa Water

Arran Heritage Museum

South Beach

Glen Cloy Rd

Auchrannie Rd

Golf course

Auchrannie Spa

Auchrannie House Hotel

Co-op

Alma Rd

Book & Card Centre

Co-op

Arran Active

Little Rock café

Douglas Hotel

Ardrossan – Brodick ferry

Pier

Bus station

Market Rd

Strathwhillan Rd

A841

The name Brodick comes from the Norse 'breda-vick' or broad bay, the backdrop to Arran's second largest village. Brodick Pier has a helpful VisitScotland iCentre: see page 74 for contact details. There's a wide range of accommodation, including the superb Auchrannie House Hotel, Country Club & Spa (01770 302 234 www.auchrannie.co.uk) and the finely refurbished Douglas Hotel.

Brodick has some excellemt shops, including a group beside the Mini Golf: Arran Active for outdoor gear, Arran Ice Cream and Bunty's gift shop plus the excellent Little Rock café. (open 9.00-17.00). The Book & Card Centre is just along the road. The Arran Brewery is a micro-brewery at Cladach offering tours and tastings: 01770 302 353, www.arranbrewery.com. There's also Arran Aromatics (www.arranaromatics.com) and the Island Cheese Company (www.islandcheese.co.uk), both at Duchess Court. See also pages 32-33 for the Arran Heritage Museum and Brodick Castle.

Isle of Arran Heritage Museum

This museum opened in 1979 on the site of a small school, in buildings that were a croft, smiddy, farmhouse, dairy and stables. It displays a comprehensive collection about Arran's social history, people, culture and geology. Its lovely grounds descend to the Rosa Burn, and outdoor exhibits include farm machinery, a restored Brodick bathing hut and an antique petrol pump (right). The Cottage has parlour, bedroom, kitchen, wash house and milk house, all furnished to display details of domestic life in the early 20th century, using items donated by local residents and visitors.

Other buildings house recreated interiors – a post office with antique telephone exchange, a 1920s classroom and a smiddy with original forges, bellows and tools. From time to time a blacksmith demonstrates his art in the working smiddy. There are specialist sections on geology, archaeology and genealogy, with extensive displays and some audiovisuals. The Café Rosaburn offers light meals, snacks and home baking.

In 2017 entry to the museum and gardens cost £4 (concessions £3, gardens and café only adults £0.50). The museum is open daily 10.30-16.30, generally from the end of March to the end to October, but check: visit *www.arranmuseum.co.uk* or tel 01770 302 636.

Restored farm machinery

Parlour in the Cottage

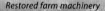

Brodick Castle

Arran's most popular tourist attraction is a rare example of a medieval defensive castle that later became a Victorian family country house. From 1503 the castle (and much of the island) belonged to the Dukes of Hamilton. In 1844 the 10th Duke commissioned architect James Gillespie Graham to extend and transform the castle into a gracious home for his eldest son, who had just married Princess Marie of Baden.

Castle gate

In 1906 the 12th Duke's only child, Lady Mary Louise Hamilton married the 6th Duke of Montrose, and the interior that you see today strongly reflects their interests and tastes. She and her son-in-law Major Boscawen were responsible for redesigning the gardens, which feature superb rhododendrons, four summer houses, gorges and waterfalls, a walled garden and an ice house.

Following the death of Mary, Duchess of Montrose, in 1957, the castle and gardens were passed to the National Trust for Scotland (in lieu of death duties). Her surviving daughter, Lady Jean Fforde, continues to live in Brodick and wrote the Foreword to the excellent NTS guidebook on the castle. A wide range of good paintings, photographs, sporting trophies and objets d'art are displayed in the private apartments. The domestic details of the kitchen and servants' quarters are equally interesting.

The Castle was closed in 2017 for improvements, but from 2018 is due to reopen daily from 11.00, Easter to October; the Country Park opens year-round from 09.30 to sunset. In 2016, castle admission cost £12.50 per adult, £9 per concession: tel 01770 302 202. There are helpful staff in each room, but your visit is self-guided. Discover more from the National Trust for Scotland website: *www.nts.org.uk*.

Brodick Castle from its walled garden

Glenrosa Water

North over Brodick

Putting green

Co-op

3·2 Brodick to Sannox

Distance	7·8 miles 12·6 km
Terrain	pavement, footpath, cycle tracks through Merkland Wood and some path leading to road-walking beside the A841; the high-level option takes you on mountain paths to the shoulder, or summit, of Goat Fell
Grade	main route climbs steadily to 180 m/590 ft, then levels and descends to the road fairly gently; the Goat Fell alternative climbs to 630 m/2050 ft (shoulder) or 874 m/2870 ft for the summit
Food & drink	Brodick (choice), Cladach (bar and bistro), Corrie (shop and hotel), Sannox (hotel and bar)
Side-trip	optional climb of extra 244 m/800 ft to summit: see page 38
Summary	a potentially strenuous first day, with a big altitude gain and loss by the Goat Fell route, rewarded by amazing 360° views; in poor weather, choose the low-level alternative

Goat Fell

Brodick	2·3	3·3	2·2	Sannox
	3·7	5·3	3·6	

- Start from the ferry terminal, and walk along the beachside pavement west through Brodick for about 1 km, leaving the main road at the putting green to pick up the Fisherman's Walk.

- The Walk sticks to the coastline, whilst the main road goes inland. The Way now crosses three footbridges over streams, the first one very soon on your left. After crossing it, follow the boardwalk north **1**, eventually to cross the golf course. Give way to golfers (and beware of golf balls) from here on.

- After 600 m, cross the golf club's metal footbridge over Glenrosa Water. **2** Turn right *immediately* to follow the path downstream.

- After 500 m, look for the discreet waymarker **3** pointing you left along a gorse-lined path leading to Brodick's north beach. Behind you there are lovely views over Brodick Bay. Goat Fell towers above you ahead, whilst Brodick Castle nestles in the trees ahead.

- At the end of the beach, cross the timber footbridge and follow the path past the Mountain Rescue Post. Cross the main road with care to reach the Cladach Visitor Centre with its cluster of shops.

- Walk through the car park and past the footpath to Brodick Castle to the Goat Fell track, marked by a timber post. (The choice point between Goat Fell and the main Way comes a little later.) Follow the wide track gently uphill, at first lined with fine mature trees.

- Ignore various other trails signed to left and right, keeping to the main track until it sweeps around to the right, now a broad forest road, labelled 'Balmoral Ride' and waymarked Arran Coastal Way.

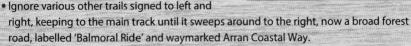

- Here you choose: for the low-level route, follow the road around to the right and pass through a gate. For the Goat Fell alternative, skip to page 38.

- The main Way follows the forest road east as it climbs gently through woodland. After it descends and crosses the Merkland Burn, you reach a waymarked fingerpost which announces 'Corrie 2·5 miles/4 km'. This is 1·6 km after you left the Goat Fell track.

- Turn left and follow this track all the way to Corrie. At first it climbs gently, passing through dense forest on a broad, smooth forest road. This reaches a large clearing with a bench where you can enjoy fine views over the Firth of Clyde, with the island of Little Cumbrae to the north-east.

- After the clearing, the track narrows and becomes much bumpier, undulating gently through dense woodland. Plashing streams and peat-laden pools adorn the trackside, and a few breaks in the trees provide glimpses of the Clyde and the Arran shore around Corrie.

- After snaking your way downhill, you start to hear traffic from the A841 and descend all the way to meet the main road where you turn left. After 300 m, you pass a sign on the left where the Goat Fell route rejoins you. Walk a further 1 km (0·6 miles) to reach Corrie: see page 39.

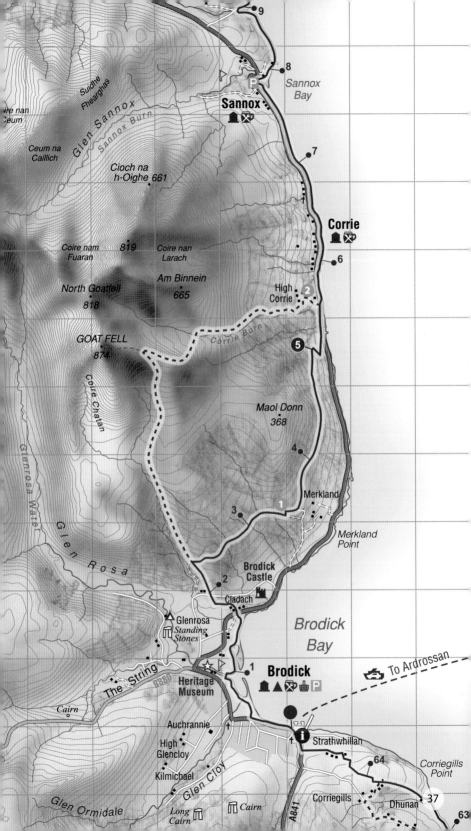

Sannox Bay

Sannox

9

8

7

Corrie

High Corrie

2

5

6

Suidhe Fhearghas

Glen Sannox

Sannox Burn

re nan eum

Ceum na Caillich

Cioch na h-Oighe 661

Coire nam Fuaran

819

Coire nan Larach

Am Binnein 665

North Goatfell 818

GOAT FELL 874

Coire Lan

Corrie Burn

Maol Donn 368

4

Merkland

1

3

Merkland Point

Brodick Castle

Cladach

2

Glen Rosa

Glenrosa-sa Water

Glen Rosa

Glenrosa Standing Stones

1

Brodick Bay

Brodick

To Ardrossan

The String

B880

Heritage Museum

Cairn

Auchrannie

High Glencloy

Kilmichael

Glen Cloy

Strathwhillan

64

Corriegills Point

Corriegills

Dhunan

37

Glen Ormidale

Long Cairn

Cairn

A841

63

The Goat Fell alternative

At the junction mentioned above, bear left (north-west) on the narrow Goat Fell path which climbs steadily and crosses a number of streams. Go through a tall timber gate in the deer fence to enter land managed by the National Trust for Scotland (NTS). There are great views behind you to Holy Isle and the Ayrshire coast.

The path continues to climb, in places steeply, heading northerly towards a ridge. You must identify this ridge, which runs west-east, to find the junction with your descent path to Corrie, about 2 km from the deer fence, at altitude 630 m, grid reference NR 997 415.

The 2015 OS Explorer map still shows a cairn at this path junction, but it was removed many years ago, and the NTS still does not permit cairns. The two paths (from Brodick and to Corrie) merge at an angle of about 30 degrees: the photograph below should help.

Depending on the conditions, your energy level and the time available before dark, this is your choice point. If in doubt, head straight down to Corrie, almost easterly at first. However, if you are tempted and can spare at least two hours for the round trip, read on before deciding.

On a fine day, Goat Fell's summit (at 874 m/2868 ft) offers richly rewarding 360° views and could be the highlight of your entire trip. The ascent of a further 244 m/800 ft above the path junction takes most people about 30-45 minutes. The trail is narrow and rocky, a bit steeper and more strenuous than before, but in good conditions there is nothing to deter a hill-walker with any enthusiasm.

Once you reach the spacious granite summit, a location finder plate identifies not only the mountains of north Arran nearby, but also distant views of Jura, the Kintyre and Cowal peninsulas, the Clyde islands of Bute and the Cumbraes, the Ayrshire coast, Ailsa Craig and the coast of Northern Ireland. On a clear day, many mountains of mainland Scotland may be seen – from Ben Lomond (45 miles/72 km) all the way to Ben Lawers, some 74 miles/120 km away.

Junction between the paths, seen from above

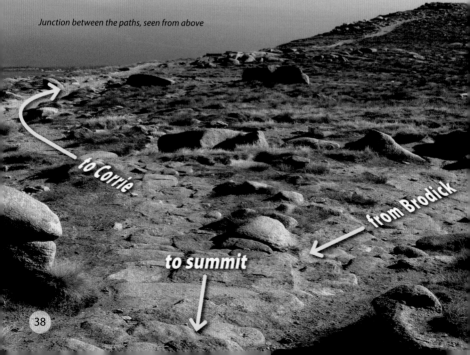

to Corrie

from Brodick

to summit

North from Goat Fell's summit

After enjoying the view, take care to descend by the way you came, leaving the summit area south then east, and looking out for the path junction at NR 997 415. Now bear left, descending the rough boulder-strewn ridge that heads east-south-east at first, towards Corrie. There's a couple of awkward steps where you may prefer to use your hands.

After about 700 m, the path swings to the left, northerly, and becomes more heathery as it descends to the Corrie Burn. Cross it by stepping-stones, with care if it is in spate. On its far side, a clear broad path descends from your left, leading down from North Goat Fell.

Turn right (east) down this path that follows the burn downstream, at first across open hillside. En route, you climb a ladder stile, go through a kissing-gate and cross various streams. The path becomes pleasantly surrounded by heather, bracken and bog myrtle, and eventually meets a broad, rough track.

Bear left down the track, which soon becomes metalled, and after 500 m passes High Corrie, and drops steeply to meet the main road. Turn left, passing a bus stop to reach Corrie's village centre within 1 km.

- Walking north along the right of the main road, the journey through Corrie to Sannox is full of interest, both in geology and marine life. The rock formations are wonderful, both on the beach and roadside, and Corrie's wooden seal statue reminds you to look out for real ones, basking on the rocks. You'll also see sea birds and possibly even a basking shark if the sea is calm: see page 27.

- You will pass the Corrie and Sannox Village Hall, two small harbours, shops, the Rock Pool café and the Corrie Hotel with Ferry Rock opposite. Around the bend in the road, pass the church and primary school, and after 1 km you enter Sannox, with a Sannox Bay information board, quay and Sannox Bay Hotel. Today's walk ends at the car park at the northern end of Sannox, where buses also stop.

3·3 Sannox to Lochranza

Distance	9·8 miles 15·7 km	
Terrain	rocky sections with easy scrambling; path muddy in places, especially after rain; stepped path makes boulder field passable at all states of tide	
Grade	coastal path with negligible altitude gain, but the terrain make it strenuous, especially in wet conditions	
Food & drink	Sannox (hotel and bar), Lochranza (sandwich bar and hotel)	
Summary	a glorious day of off-road coastal walking, with many points of interest; in normal conditions, thanks to path improvements, this section is no longer too challenging	

```
          2·2              2·7           1·7            3·2
O──────────────────O────────────────O───────O──────────────────O
Sannox   3·6   Fallen Rocks  4·3  Laggan Cottage  2·7  An Scriodan  5·1   Lochranza
```

- Just beyond the car park on the right, look for the waymarked fingerpost 'North Sannox' that points straight across Sannox Burn by concrete cuboid stepping stones. The route seems to lead directly to the beach, but, just before, it turns left along a sandy path between gorse bushes, parallel to the shore.

- The path passes the garden gates of a few houses, and at first seems narrowly channelled between hedge and fence. You pass a tall white post, the southern end of the Sannox Measured Mile, which many famous ships have used for their time trials. The path broadens out and runs parallel to a cliff face.

- About 1 mile (1·6 km) north of Sannox you need to cross North Sannox Burn. Follow the waymarkers inland and cross by the bridge, afterwards heading right on the minor road back to the picnic area near the coast.

Fallen Rocks

- Pass through a gate, along a pleasantly wooded path with intermittent sea views, and large boulders to the left. After a picnic bench, you get your first glimpse of Fallen Rocks, an impressive landslip where colossal boulders tumbled from the cliffs to the sea. However there's no difficulty about picking your way through.

- Later the path opens out, with bracken-covered hills set back to the left and wide, open views over the Firth of Clyde to your right, with the islands of Bute and the Cumbraes prominent. There are fine rock formations in this section, and also some caves up to your left.

- About 2·5 miles (4 km) after Fallen Rocks, you reach the wonderfully isolated white cottage at Laggan. The Way keeps right along the shore, within 800 m reaching the ruins of Duchess Anne's Salt Pan.

Laggan Cottage

Built in 1710, this Salt Pan fell into disuse after only 20 years. Salt was vital to preserve meat and fish, and heavily taxed by the government. The discovery of coal nearby made it possible to extract the salt from seawater. Arran salt was particularly pure, but the process proved uneconomic. The ruined building below is the pan-house, where the furnace and iron pans were. Smaller buildings nearby (of which traces remain) stored fuel and salt, with workers' cottages inland. Coal was dug from scattered pits, now water-filled.

Duchess Anne's Salt Pan

- One mile (1·6 km) after the Salt Pan, you reach the Cock of Arran, named after a huge sandstone boulder which, before its head fell off, resembled a crowing cockerel. There are caves up to the left, one known as Ossian's Cave or the Picture Cave, with ship carvings and dates.

- Beyond the Cock lies An Scriodan Rock Fall ❶, a boulder-field that makes for slow, strenuous going. This section has been greatly improved by major works to convert the largest single obstacle into a rock staircase. However, expect slow progress and take great care if traversing this section in the wet. Slipping could lead to an ankle-wrenching fall.

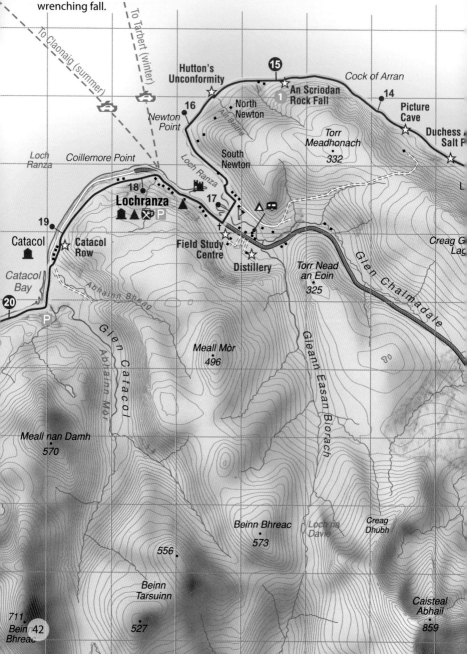

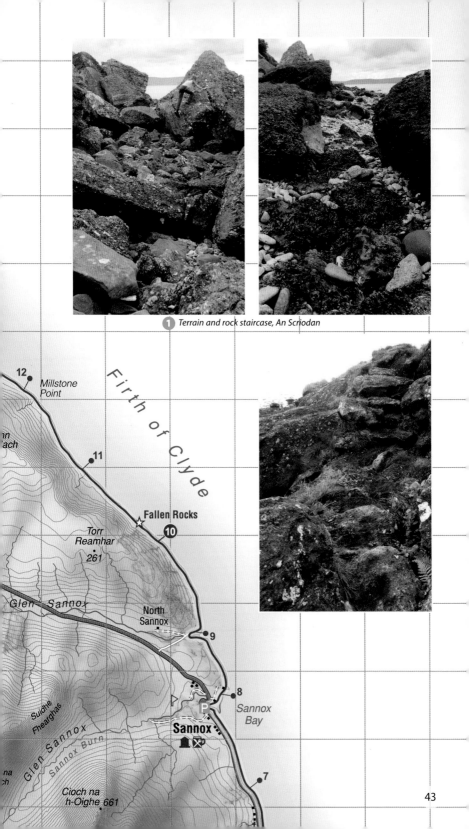

1 *Terrain and rock staircase, An Scriodan*

Firth of Clyde

12 Millstone Point

11

Fallen Rocks ☆
10

Torr Reamhar
·261

Glen Sannox

North Sannox
9

8

🅿 Sannox Bay

Sannox

Suidhe Fhearghas

Glen Sannox

Sannox Burn

7

Cioch na h-Oighe 661

43

- After An Scriodan, you pass a whitewashed stone cottage (Fairy Dell) and shingle beach gives way to a mostly grassy path. Soon you start to see the headland beyond Lochranza. You're approaching Hutton's Unconformity, the geological feature noticed by James Hutton in 1787: see page 17. The path turns right towards the shore, and at a waymarker post the Way turns left to resume the coast towards Newton Point.

- Here, instead turn right for 10 m on a faint trod path to reach the best viewpoint for the Unconformity, looking across the stream (Allt Beithe) which reaches the shore here: see the photo below, taken at high tide. The Unconformity is not marked on either OS or Harvey maps, but its grid reference is NR 936 521. Happily, in late 2017 a disc was finally being added to this waymarker post as part of the Arran Geopark project. Until then, most people saw nothing on the ground and walked past, oblivious to this landmark.

- After the Unconformity, follow the constructed path south-west for 600 m to reach Newton Point: keep to the rocky shoreline to avoid the boggy saltmarsh of the raised beach. The Point has a good location finder, dedicated to 'those who have done so much for geology and walking on Arran'. (However, it overstates the distance to Hutton's Unconformity as half a mile.)

Hutton's Angular Unconformity

- The path leads to a minor road that after 800 m turns right, skirting Loch Ranza to rejoin the main road. Turn right to continue the Way, or left to visit the distillery with Casks Café: see page 22. The distillery tour is recommended, but must be booked in advance.

Lochranza is Arran's most northerly village, linked in summer by ferry to Claonaig, on Kintyre. Its ruined castle enhances its situation. Surrounded by hills and facing north-east, it holds the British record for the shortest hours of sunshine in December.

Visitors will probably remember it as the place where wild red deer appear to wander around fearlessly. Seals bask on the rocks of Loch Ranza's shores, and the coast is rich in flowers and sea birds. With a Field Studies Centre and Youth Hostel, the village often hosts groups of geology students from afar.

Lochranza Castle from the east

Distillery entrance: a former still

Lochranza Castle

The original castle was built for the MacSweens in the early 13th century, like Skipness Castle to help guard the Kilbrannan Sound. Most of the present ruins result from the C16th rebuilding. Allegedly, Robert the Bruce landed here in 1306 from Ireland, en route to his successful bid for the Scottish Crown.

The castle changed hands repeatedly, being extended, modified and fortified. In the 15-17th centuries, it belonged to the Earls of Montgomery. In the 1650s Cromwell put a garrison here, and in 1705 it passed to the Hamiltons. For visit information, check **www.historicenvironment.scot.**

3·4 Lochranza to Imachar

Distance	8·9 miles 14·3 km
Terrain	hill path at first, then mainly road-walking, taking to the verge or beach in places; the last 2 miles (3·2 km) are excellent beach-walking
Grade	Postman's Walk rises to 70 m (230 ft), then descends to the coast at Catacol, from where the Way remains almost at sea level
Food & drink	Lochranza (shop, hotel), Catacol (hotel), Pirnmill (tea room)
Side-trip	Coire Lochan: see panel on page 49
Summary	most walkers will relish the off-road start and finish of the day, but some walkers may not enjoy the long (5 mi/8 km) stretch of road walking in between, though traffic is light, and the views good

1·9		4·4		2·6	
Lochranza	3·0 Catacol	7·1		Pirnmill	4·2 Imachar

- From the T-junction, follow the main road north-west around the loch, past the Field Studies Centre and Youth Hostel. To visit the ruins of Lochranza Castle, turn right along its curved grassy spit: see the panel on page 45.

- Continue along the road past the hotel, then at the sign 'Claonaig ferry 115 yards' turn left up the farm track as waymarked. The track climbs steadily towards Coillemore Farm, which includes parts of the oldest surviving house in Arran (built 1500-1700). Look behind you for views of Newton Point and Loch Ranza: see photo below.

- After 280 m, turn right off the track to follow the 'Postman's Walk' for the next 1·3 miles/2·1 km. The narrow grassy path heads steeply uphill at first, bearing left towards a telegraph pole. It then undulates gently through birch woodland, at first on a constructed section of path which helps your progress above the sodden terrain. In places, you have good views to your right across the Kilbrannan Sound to Kintyre.

Constructed path

Ferry from Claonaig approaching Lochranza

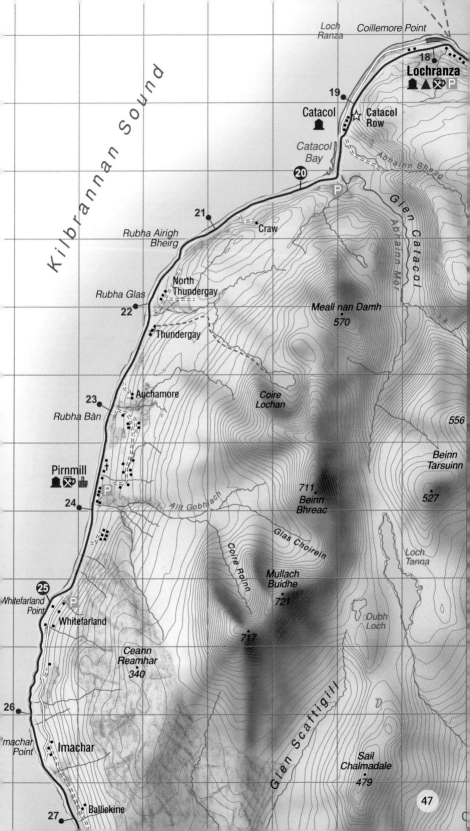

Loch Ranza
Coillemore Point

Lochranza 18

Catacol 19
Catacol Row

Catacol Bay

20

21
Craw

Rubha Airigh Bheirg

North Thundergay

Rubha Glas 22

Thundergay

K i l b r a n n a n   S o u n d

Meall nan Damh
570

Coire Lochan

G l e n   C a t a c o l

Abhainn Bheag

Abhainn Mòr

Auchamore 23

Rubha Bàn

556

Beinn Tarsuinn

Pirnmill

24

Allt Gobhlach

Beinn Bhreac
711

527

Glas Choirein

Coire Roinn

Mullach Buidhe
721

Loch Tanna

717

Dubh Loch

25
Whitefarland Point
Whitefarland

Ceann Reamhar
340

26

G l e n   S c a f t i g i l l

machar Point
Imachar

Sail Chalmadale
479

47

27
Balliekine

Obstacles on the Postman's Path

- Once the constructed section gives out, however, the going is slow – boggy in places, with bracken, tree roots, rocks and a few streams to cross. There are a couple of fallen tree trunks to climb over, and low branches to squeeze under. In places the path is indistinct, marked only by occasional splashes of yellow paint. Be aware of the steep drop to your right, overgrown in many places.

- Eventually you emerge from woodland to gain your first clear view of Catacol Bay. 'Catacol' is Old Norse for 'the valley of the cat' and you are about to descend to the floor of steep-sided Glen Catacol. The village features Catacol Row – 12 white houses known as 'The Apostles' – and the Catacol Bay Hotel.

- Keep to the path which does not descend until it's above the far end of Catacol Row. It then drops steeply to a tall ladder stile. Beyond the stile, turn right at the farm road to reach the main road, where the Way continues to the left. First, make a small detour to your right, to see Catacol Row and perhaps to visit the Catacol Bay Hotel just beyond.

Tall ladder stile

Catacol Row

- The Row was built in the mid-19th century after Lord Rossmore had burnt his tenants out of their homes at Old Catacol to make way for deer stalking. The displaced crofters rejected the houses and dispersed around the island, whilst the houses stood empty until other tenants could be found. Each of the the 12 Apostles has a different window design, the theory being that fishermen's wives could signal with oil lamps to their husbands while they were out in their boats.

- Continue south on the main road, crossing it to face oncoming traffic. (You can take to the beach briefly here, but soon must cross a stream.)

- After Catacol Bay, the road crosses a river, the Abhainn Mor, undulating and twisting, with poor sight lines: walk with care. Two miles beyond the river, follow waymarkers to take to the beach, but only for 500 m. Look out for rugged rock formations and caves on the left.

- The signpost to the Coire Lochan side-trip is at about mile 22·2: see panel. From here it's 1·5 miles (2·4 km) to the scattered village of Pirnmill. Its name derives from the pirns, or bobbins, manufactured here. The tall thin house where they were made stands inland, after the cafe and shop. After Pirnmill Primary School, walk one mile (1·6 km) further towards Whitefarland, where you finally leave the road, 5 miles (8 km) after Catacol.

Coire Fhion Lochan

Three miles (5 km) after Catacol, a signposted path leads off left from Mid Thundergay to what is, in good weather, a lovely excursion to Coire Lochan. This small oval lochan is encircled by hills, with beautiful views to the west. The signpost leads to an access track where you follow signage through the kissing-gate. Follow the clear footpath for 800 m to go over a ladder stile and across a burn. The route swings south-easterly and goes upstream alongside the burn to the shores of its source. It's a stiff climb to 330 m (1100 ft) and about 4 miles (6·4 km) round trip: allow at least two hours.

- At mile 24·7, pass a car park (on the left) and 150 m later bear right just before the children's swings where a waymarker soon confirms the beginning of the offroad path. This leads to the beach where you are free to choose from whichever surfaces – shingle, rock or sand – are on offer

West over Coire Lochan

Burial ground on the beach south of Pirnmill

- After about 800 m, a pile of rocks marks an interesting walled graveyard on the left, which you can explore by climbing in from either side. Central in the photograph, the lichen-covered gravestone is to Captain John McMillan who died 1884 aged 48, erected by his widow.

- An intermittent path may give easier going than the beach, but in places you may have to negotiate slippery rocks. There's a fine stretch of grassy path in a wide flat section below the cliffs, and you'll see a couple of caves on the left.

- Throughout this beach walk, Kintyre's coast seems very close: from Imachar Point, to Carradale is barely 3 miles (5 km). A ferry used to ply from Imachar to Carradale and (to its south) Saddell Abbey.

- Near the end of the beach section, pass over two stiles, and rejoin the main road at a sharp bend that marks the end of this section.

- You are about 2·5 miles (4 km) south of Pirnmill and could walk back or, if you've timed your walk well, catch a bus to accommodation there or elsewhere. If flagging down a bus, stand somewhere that gives clear sight lines to the traffic, on the correct side of the road for your intended direction.

Kintyre's coast from near Imachar Point

3·5 Imachar to Blackwaterfoot

Distance	10·0 miles 16·1 km	
Terrain	mainly road-walking, followed by a delightful beach path that emerges at Blackwaterfoot	
Grade	coastal road remains almost at sea level; once off-road, there's a slight climb (to 70 m/230 ft) and descent before the King's Cave, then the path stays on or close to the beach	
Food & drink	Machrie (tea room), Blackwaterfoot (golf club, hotel, bakery)	
Side-trip	Machrie Moor Stone Circles: see page 18	
Summary	road-walking for 6 miles (10 km), then a splendid coastal path past Drumadoon Point to Blackwaterfoot	

Stone circle

Imachar	2·5	Iorsa Water	2·7	Machrie	1·1	Car park	3·7	Blackwaterfoot
	4·0		4·3		1·8		6·0	

- From the bend in the road near Imachar, continue south along the main road, using the verge on the right whenever gorse and brambles permit. In places, you may prefer to take to the beach as appropriate. The views are dominated by the cliffs of Drumadoon Point ahead, with Kintyre to your right, and usually there are seabirds on the water.

- After Dougarie Lodge, an imposing white building with step gables, cross the Iorsa Water. (Within 1 km, there is the option to detour to the Old Byre with Café Thyme.) Soon after, you start to see impressive caves on the raised beach to your left, formed by the sea some 10,000 years ago in Devonian sandstone.

- Further south you'll see more cliffs, also set back from the road. At a road junction 4 miles (6·4 km) after Imachar, bear left to detour to Auchagallon Stone Circle. Otherwise, stay on the main road, approaching the Machrie Moor Stone Circles side-trip: see page 18. You could fortify yourself first with fresh local baking from the Machrie Tea Room (by Machrie Golf Club), just between this road junction and Machrie Water.

- After the Machrie Moor junction, it's almost 1 mile (1·6 km) to the car park with picnic area where the Way finally leaves the main road. The information board shows both the Way to the King's Cave and a newer return path for those making a circular walk. Bear right along the signed path north-westerly, enjoying great views over Machrie Bay towards Beinn Bharrain.

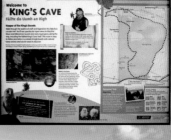

The path soon descends steeply by a rocky gully to pass through a gate and reach the beach. Follow the intermittent path along the foreshore, picking the easiest route among the rocks depending on the tide.

You will start to notice former sea caves on your left. The King's Cave is reached by a path with unmistakable stone steps and ornate ironwork railings.

This palatial cave is alleged to have been used in 1307 by Robert the Bruce en route from Ireland to the Scottish mainland. Although his famous spider encounter probably took place elsewhere, if at all, the cave is of great interest for its ancient rock carvings, some dating from the Iron Age and possibly even Bronze Age. There are intriguing animal images, Ogham inscriptions and Christian symbols. For photographs, visit our web page *www.rucsacs.com/links/acw*.

2 *The King's Cave*

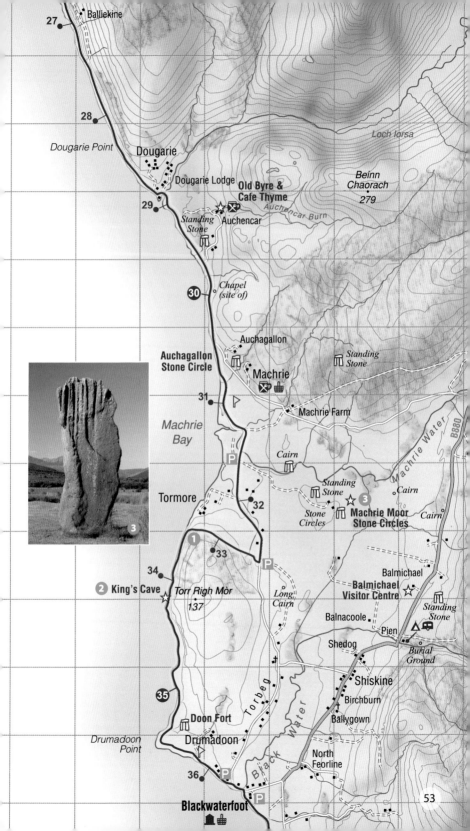

27 Balliekine

28

Dougarie Point

Dougarie

Dougarie Lodge

Old Byre & Cafe Thyme

Auchencar Burn

Beinn Chaorach
279

Loch Iorsa

29

Standing Stone

Auchencar

30

Chapel (site of)

Auchagallon

Auchagallon Stone Circle

Standing Stone

Machrie

31

Machrie Bay

Machrie Farm

Cairn

P

Tormore

Standing Stone

Cairn

32

Stone Circles

Machrie Moor Stone Circles

3

Cairn

Machrie Water

B880

1

33

P

Balmichael

34

2 King's Cave

Torr Righ Mòr
137

Long Cairn

Balmichael Visitor Centre

Standing Stone

Balnacoole

Pien

Shedog

Burial Ground

35

Shiskine

Torbeg

Birchburn

Doon Fort

Ballygown

Drumadoon Point

Drumadoon

Black Water

North Feorline

36

P

Blackwaterfoot

P

53

3

Rocky coast on the approach to Drumadoon Point

- About 800 m after the cave, a huge rock stands on its own in a grassy clearing. It bears the footprints of a Triassic lizard-like dinosaur (Chirotherium barthii), some 200-240 million years old. There are great views across to Campbeltown with Davaar Island, and of Kintyre's southern tip, with Sanda, the 'spoon' island.

- Shortly after the footprints, there's a field decorated with strange piles of stones, a playful man-made addition to Arran's geology. To continue the Way, turn right at a path junction and keep to the coast (signed for Blackwaterfoot) which soon approaches the imposing cliffs on which Doon (or Drumadoon) Fort is perched.

Miniature cairns beside the path

- The sheer cliffs of Drumadoon Point look increasingly dramatic as you approach. They're about 60 million years old, known to geologists as a great example of a Tertiary sill. The rough path threads its way along the grass and boulders at the foot of these cliffs.

Cliffs of Drumadoon Point: a Tertiary sill

- After the cliffs, the path goes around the headland, passing through an impressive gap blasted through enormous rocks, so as to circumnavigate Shiskine Golf Course, which sits above the foreshore. Go around Drumadoon Point and cross the golden sands of one of Arran's most delightful beaches.

- After 1 km of beach, head uphill to the car park and follow the minor road which soon joins the main road and crosses the Black Water. On the far side of the bridge, turn right into the main village of Blackwaterfoot, soon reaching the Best Western Kinloch Hotel. This may be a welcome stop for refreshments and overnight: in addition to bar meals, the hotel has a tempting bakery at its back.

Path below Shiskine Golf Course

Blackwaterfoot's sandy beach

Distance	6·6 miles 10·7 km		
Terrain	after a few miles of walking on the beach, the main Way heads up to the road, or you can opt for more coastal walking, in places on boggy and broken ground		
Grade	fairly flat along path, then (main Way) a minor climb on road to Sliddery and undulations to reach Lagg; coastal route flat until it climbs to rejoin the road at Sliddery		
Food & drink	Blackwaterfoot (golf club, hotel and bakery), Lagg Hotel		
Summary	this short section starts on coastal path, then offers a choice of easy going on road or tougher conditions underfoot if you stay coastal; either way, the sea views are splendid		

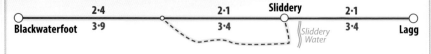

Blackwaterfoot	2·4 / 3·9	2·1 / 3·4	Sliddery / Sliddery Water	2·1 / 3·4	Lagg

- Pass between the Kinloch Hotel and the beach along a minor road. After passing a few houses the road gives way to a broad, stony path. Keep heading south around the bay, using the beach as appropriate and crossing streams by stepping stones. Look behind for great views back across Drumadoon Bay and its beaches, with mountains beyond.

- You are approaching a headland, Kilpatrick Point, at first by a grassy path, sometimes overgrown with bracken and brambles. Once you've rounded the point, look out for three caves close together in the cliffs to your left. This is about 1 mile (1·6 km) after the bridge over the Black Water.

- The middle one is known as the Preaching Cave. It was used from 1815-21 instead of the parish church, by a congregation who didn't like the minister imposed on them. Instead, they chose to worship in this cave, led by one of their own elders.

Grassy path near Kilpatrick Point

- There's a tortuous path through the vegetation, with only the occasional waymarker to reassure you that you are still on course. Using a mixture of rock-hopping and path-finding, pass around one small headland after another.

Across Drumadoon Bay to Blackwaterfoot

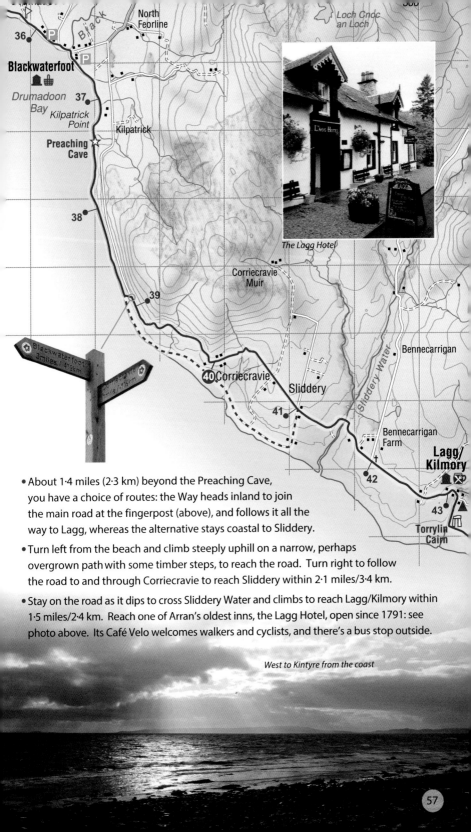

The Lagg Hotel

- About 1·4 miles (2·3 km) beyond the Preaching Cave, you have a choice of routes: the Way heads inland to join the main road at the fingerpost (above), and follows it all the way to Lagg, whereas the alternative stays coastal to Sliddery.

- Turn left from the beach and climb steeply uphill on a narrow, perhaps overgrown path with some timber steps, to reach the road. Turn right to follow the road to and through Corriecravie to reach Sliddery within 2·1 miles/3·4 km.

- Stay on the road as it dips to cross Sliddery Water and climbs to reach Lagg/Kilmory within 1·5 miles/2·4 km. Reach one of Arran's oldest inns, the Lagg Hotel, open since 1791: see photo above. Its Café Velo welcomes walkers and cyclists, and there's a bus stop outside.

West to Kintyre from the coast

Coastal alternative

Track leading to Sliddery

The coastal option is similar in distance, but much slower going because of the rough terrain, much of it cattle-churned and stony, and it can be extremely boggy. Avoid choosing this option during or just after wet weather. The rock and bracken foreshore gives way to fenced fields, fringed by a gravelly shore. Stick to the water-side, below the fences.

The coastal views are glorious. The volcanic plug of Ailsa Craig, distant to the south, signals that you have 'rounded the corner' of Arran. To the west lie the hills of Kintyre and Davaar Island. The dark basalt dykes are often adorned at low tide with basking seals.

Follow a track that winds through the disused gravel quarry. Pass between two timber posts standing beside a gate, and walk along the beach past the next field.

After a slow 2·2 miles (3·6 km), regain the road by turning left up the track towards two stone houses. The track climbs between fenced fields to meet the main road at Sliddery's bus stop. Turn right along the road to reach Lagg.

South towards Galloway, with Ailsa Craig at left

3·7 Lagg to Whiting Bay

60 61 63

Distance	11·3 miles 18·3 km
Terrain	after a little road, this begins with beach walking, then involves one or two boulder-fields and headlands that are impassable at high tide: read on before deciding which option
Grade	no altitude gain on the coastal route, but strenuous boulder-hopping; the main Way avoids Dippin Head by going inland, climbing to 230 m/750 ft and descending steeply from Glenashdale Falls to the coast
Food & drink	Lagg Hotel, Kildonan (short detour), Whiting Bay
Summary	this section demands tidal awareness and sensible planning, richly rewarded by untamed scenery and spectacular seascapes; adventurous walkers will prefer the coastal option, but in poor weather or at adverse tide times, the inland Way is attractive

escape route

Whiting Bay

2·4   2·9   1·0 A841   3·2   Falls   1·8

Lagg   3·9   4·7   1·6   5·2   2·9

coastal (Dippin Head)

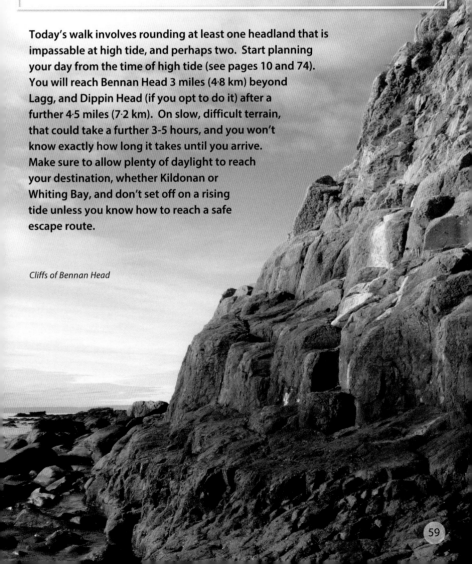

Today's walk involves rounding at least one headland that is impassable at high tide, and perhaps two. Start planning your day from the time of high tide (see pages 10 and 74). You will reach Bennan Head 3 miles (4·8 km) beyond Lagg, and Dippin Head (if you opt to do it) after a further 4·5 miles (7·2 km). On slow, difficult terrain, that could take a further 3-5 hours, and you won't know exactly how long it takes until you arrive. Make sure to allow plenty of daylight to reach your destination, whether Kildonan or Whiting Bay, and don't set off on a rising tide unless you know how to reach a safe escape route.

Cliffs of Bennan Head

59

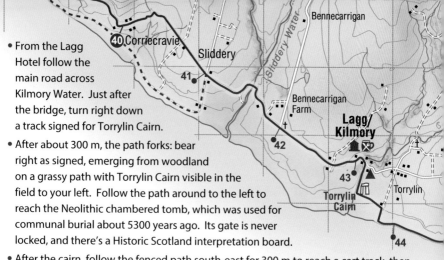

- From the Lagg Hotel follow the main road across Kilmory Water. Just after the bridge, turn right down a track signed for Torrylin Cairn.

- After about 300 m, the path forks: bear right as signed, emerging from woodland on a grassy path with Torrylin Cairn visible in the field to your left. Follow the path around to the left to reach the Neolithic chambered tomb, which was used for communal burial about 5300 years ago. Its gate is never locked, and there's a Historic Scotland interpretation board.

- After the cairn, follow the fenced path south-east for 300 m to reach a cart track, then turn right down to the beach. Enjoy some of the easiest beach-walking so far, with firm sand and lovely views to the south, towards Ailsa Craig.

- Cross a low timber stile on a grassy trod path above the boulders and dykes. The going gets tougher and you have to pick your way through broken, boggy ground. After the second stile (waymarked) you begin to see dark cliffs ahead and a sign soon announces 'Bennan Head & Black Cave 1·3 km, Kildonan 4·2 km'.

Easy beach-walking at mile 44

- About 800 m after the sign, a waymarked timber post shows where the escape route heads inland. Now is the time to recheck the tide time, reflect on progress and listen to your body: do you feel safe to proceed? Should you need to escape, head inland up the slope (which can be very muddy at first), turn left onto a track and follow signs to reach the main road within 1·5 km.

Walker crossing boulder-field east of Bennan Head

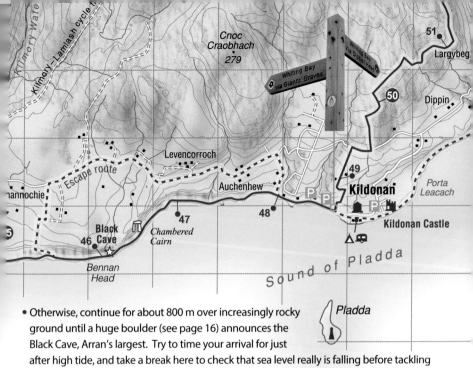

- Otherwise, continue for about 800 m over increasingly rocky ground until a huge boulder (see page 16) announces the Black Cave, Arran's largest. Try to time your arrival for just after high tide, and take a break here to check that sea level really is falling before tackling the boulders. (If conditions are worsening, or the waves and wind too great, backtrack to the escape route.)

- After the headland comes the main boulder-field: see photo on page 60. Kildonan is visible ahead, and, less than a mile offshore, Pladda with its lighthouse. There's a succession of fine basalt dykes, with seals basking and posing.

- The boulder-field gives way to a mixture of sand, rock and informal path, emerging at the minor road. Follow it along the sea front to reach the western end of Kildonan.

- Soon you will make your route choice: just past Seacrest self-catering, at a parking sign, note the fingerpost pointing left where the main Way heads inland ('Whiting Bay via Giants' Graves'), whereas the coastal alternative continues ahead.

- Whichever route you decide upon, you may wish to continue a further 500 m on the minor road to reach the Kildonan Hotel and perhaps to visit its bar and bistro. (There is also a bus stop at the drive leading to the Kildonan Hotel.) The coastal alternative goes over a longer boulder-field around Dippin Head, impassable at high tide, with no escape route. Read page 65 carefully before committing yourself to this option.

- To follow the main Way, backtrack to the fingerpost and head inland up a stony track. The track bends right behind houses and heads through a gate, confirmed by waymarkers.

Seals bask on a dyke, Pladda distant

- After 500 m from the start, turn left onto a narrow track, leaving the main track, and within 150 m turn right on a track that leads uphill to a rough road past chalets. This access road reaches the main road within 600 m.

- Turn right along the main road, taking care to face any oncoming traffic, which may be fast-moving. Within 400 m you will see a bench on the left, and a fingerpost turns you left onto a well-defined path through recently felled forestry.

- The path winds and climbs past another seat and you keep left on the track at a turning area. From here on, simply follow the main track, which becomes a forest road, ignoring all turnings and enjoying fine views. In summer, the ground is ablaze with colour, with purple heather and buddleia, yellow ragwort and deep red wild fuchsia.

Heather and saplings beside the track

- At mile 51·9, there is a fingerpost on the right marking the short detour to the Giants' Graves: see panel. Otherwise, ignore all turnings and follow the road as it snakes downhill, then veers left, inland towards Glenashdale

Forest road descending

> ### Giants' Graves
> It's only about 200 m of easy walking to reach these 5000-year-old chambered tombs. These Neolithic graves pre-date the great pyramids of Egypt and excavations have found pottery shards, flint knives, arrowheads and fragments of burnt bone. The larger one has a chamber about 6 metres long by 1 metre wide, with the smaller cairn lying about 10 m to the south, its axis at right angles. Formerly in a woodland clearing, their location now enjoys great views over Whiting Bay.

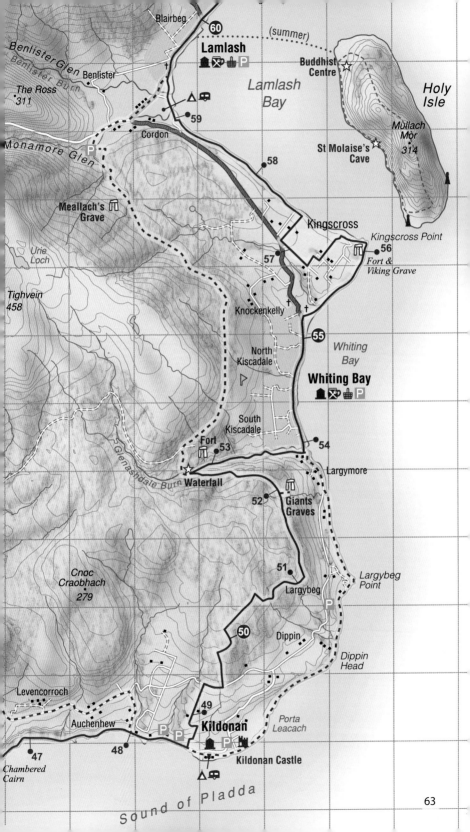

Blairbeg

60 Lamlash

(summer)

Benlister Glen

Benlister Burn

Benlister

The Ross
·311

Monamore Glen

P

59

Cordon

58

Lamlash Bay

Buddhist Centre ☆

Holy Isle

Mullach Mòr
·314

St Molaise's Cave ☆

Meallach's Grave 🗽

Urie Loch

Kingscross

Kingscross Point

Fort & Viking Grave 🗽 56

Tighvein 458

57

Knockenkelly † †

55

North Kiscadale

Whiting Bay

Whiting Bay

Glenashdale Burn

South Kiscadale

Fort 🗽 53

Waterfall ☆

54

Largymore

Giants Graves 🗽

52

Cnoc Craobhach 279

51

Largybeg

Largybeg Point

P

50

Dippin

Dippin Head

Levencorroch

Auchenhew

49

Kildonan

Porta Leacach

47

48

Kildonan Castle

Chambered Cairn

Sound of Pladda

63

At the next fingerpost, turn right to view the impressive falls where the Glenashdale Burn descends some 45 m (140 ft). Be sure to go downhill to the viewing platform which affords the view in the photograph.

If you plan to skip Whiting Bay altogether, go back up to the fingerpost and continue across the bridge on the inland alternative towards Lamlash: skip to page 70. If you are overnighting in the village, get directions from your B&B well in advance. For Viewbank Guest House, for example, you can save a lot of time and effort by staying high, crossing the bridge and descending down the east side of Glenashdale Burn.

Glenashdale Falls

- To follow the main Way down to Whiting Bay, continue down beside the burn through Glenashdale Forest. Among the great variety of trees you may see red squirrels (or at least signs of them), and a wide diversity of bird and plant life.

- The path is steep in places, but keep ahead all the way until it emerges at the main road at the southern end of Whiting Bay with bus stops, shops and cafés. It's about 2 km from here to the northern end of the village.

Coastal alternative

If you opt for Dippin Head, remember that its boulder-field is longer and more tiring than the last, with no escape route. Review the timing of high tide in the light of your progress up to now. In good conditions and without time pressure, however, this makes a superbly adventurous and rewarding choice.

Go just beyond the hotel, then descend a flight of steps to the beach. At first, the path is easy, then it combines some flat rock with grassy and stony bits. Look for the picturesque ruins of Kildonan Castle above you on a cliff. Originally a tower house, probably used more for lookout than defence, it was mainly a stronghold for the Hamilton Earls of Arran.

Cliffs of Dippin Head

The main boulder-field begins before the cliffs of Dippin Head and continues for up to an hour or so, depending on your fitness and agility. Yellow paint splashes on rocks may confirm that you are still on course.

After you round the headland, you start to see your next objective, Largybeg Point. In places, the going may be easier on the grass above the boulders, despite the brambles.

South towards Pladda from Kildonan

Basalt dyke

Progress gradually becomes easier, with smaller rocks and more of a path emerging. You still need to be vigilant: smooth rocks can be slippery when wet. There's a huge dyke and standing stones at Largybeg Point.

At the point, take the stone staircase to the top of the cliff. Reach and cross the stile, then continue parallel to the shore across the first field. Rejoin the shore and continue for a mile until you reach the main road.

After 800 m on the A841, you are joined from the left by the main Way. The road crosses the Glenashdale Burn and heads north beside the shore of Whiting Bay.

Boulder south of Largybeg Point

Approaching Largymore, with Holy Isle in clear view

3·8 Whiting Bay to Brodick

Distance 10·9 miles 17·5 km

Terrain main Way is on pavement and minor road, footpath and beach/boardwalk, inland cart track, across fields then road into Brodick; inland route is largely on forest tracks

Grade no altitude gain on the main Way (coastal) but the inland route climbs to 190 m/620 ft before descent to Lamlash; route largely flat unless you go inland from Clauchlands Point (to 150 m/490 ft)

Food & drink Whiting Bay (choice of cafés, pubs and shops), Lamlash (choice), Brodick (choice)

Summary this section starts with a choice to Lamlash – inland through forest, or coastal around Kingscross Point; the Way stays coastal almost to Brodick, but from Clauchlands Point there is a further option in case of extreme high tides

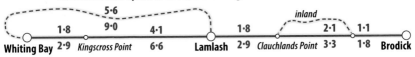

Whiting Bay · 2·9 · Kingscross Point · 1·8 · 9·0 · 5·6 · 4·1 · 6·6 · Lamlash · 1·8 · 2·9 · Clauchlands Point · inland · 2·1 · 3·3 · 1·1 · 1·8 · Brodick

The main Way is normally passable at all times. Even at an extreme high tide, there is only a short stretch between Kingscross and Cordon (south of Lamlash) that may be problematic, though at other times you may have to step carefully to avoid wet feet.

• Continue northward on the pavements of Whiting Bay to a point where the main road heads inland. Instead, turn off right at the fingerpost ('Lamlash 4·5 miles/7·5 km') along the minor road to its end. Bear right, then follow signs left across a stream and follow the coast.

• Soon the route descends (unwaymarked) to follow the beach briefly, before heading over a low stile and going inland through woodland and up timber steps to a horses' field. Pass through a timber kissing-gate (with a warning about controlling dogs because of free range hens).

• Pass through several fields and over several stiles until you see a waymarker pointing right to take you out to Kingscross Point. There's a lot of faint paths around here, but be sure to go all the way up to the rocky promontory.

• You are rewarded with an intimate view of the Holy Isle, seemingly almost close enough to touch: its lighthouse is less than 700 m away. This is a tranquil place to linger.

Kingscross Point
The sites here were first excavated by J Balfour around 1910. The large circular fort (or dun) has impressive thick circular walls skilfully built on sloping bedrock. It is probably about 2000 years old: Balfour found hearths and charcoal here, as well as iron and bone fragments. Adjacent to its south-west is a Viking grave-mound, where Balfour found burnt human bones, charcoal, rivets and nails from a boat, and a bronze coin minted in AD850. This rare example of burial by cremation in a boat probably dates from the late 13th century.

Circular fort at Kingscross Point

- Leave this area past a location finder and small cairn, heading west and staying near the coast. You pass commemorative benches and traverse the base of several fields until after 350 m the Way veers uphill into woodland. It turns sharp left, then right at a gate marked Cladach, climbing on a muddy, stony path.

- You emerge through a gap onto a farm road that heads inland for 450 m, climbing steadily beside fields, steeply in places. At its end, turn right along the minor public road, and within 100 m follow it as it turns left, then right again.

- After 450 m the road bends left to join the A841 main road, but you leave it here on a narrow path across a footbridge. Pass over a stile, through a gate and turn right to head north-east back to the coast over two footbridges.

- After over 500 m, unexpectedly you turn right down a rough road (waymarker obscure) which you leave at a gate marked 'Kilmolay'. Complete the descent to the shore on timber steps and down a steep, muddy path: take care.

- The rough, boggy coastal strip is heavily vegetated, but a series of constructed boardwalks (about 50% of the total length) eases your way through.

- Between each boardwalk section, make your way across the beach taking care on slippery seaweed and wet rocks. At low tide, the going may be easier nearer the water, but don't miss the next boardwalk: each section ends with a notice saying how far to the next one.

- Great views across to Holy Isle continue, and after you pass the offshore fish farm the view ahead opens up across Lamlash Bay with its distinctive church tower, and to the mountains beyond.

Boardwalk on coastal path

- Approaching the first houses at Cordon, start to look for the grassy area with upturned boats and a fingerpost that points inland. Turn left to walk for 70 m before turning right along a minor road parallel to the coast. Pass more houses and Middleton's Camping ground, but before the road bends left, bear right off it along a narrow path that crosses Benlister Burn by a footbridge.

- Keep straight on, soon joined by the inland route from Whiting Bay. From there, it's a further 600 m of greensward to the centre of Lamlash.

Approaching Cordon, with view of Lamlash

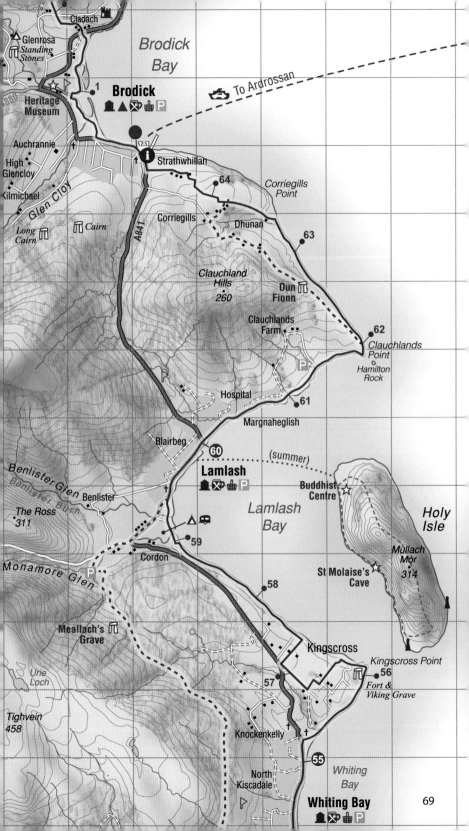

Cladach

Glenrosa
Standing
Stones

*Brodick
Bay*

To Ardrossan

Heritage
Museum

Brodick

Auchrannie

High
Glencloy

Kilmichael

Strathwhillan

64

*Corriegills
Point*

Long
Cairn

Cairn

Corriegills

Dhunan

63

Glen Cloy

*Clauchland
Hills
260*

Dun
Fionn

Clauchlands
Farm

62

*Clauchlands
Point*

*Hamilton
Rock*

Hospital

61

Benlister Glen

Benlister Burn

Blairbeg

Margnaheglish

60

(summer)

Lamlash

Buddhist
Centre

*Lamlash
Bay*

*Holy
Isle*

Benlister

The Ross
311

59

Monamore Glen

Cordon

*Mullach
Mòr
314*

St Molaise's
Cave

58

Meallach's
Grave

*Urie
Loch*

Kingscross

Kingscross Point

56

*Fort &
Viking Grave*

Tighvein
458

57

Knockenkelly

55

*Whiting
Bay*

North
Kiscadale

Whiting Bay

69

Inland alternative to Lamlash

The cycle track heading north-east

If starting from Whiting Bay, retrace your steps to go uphill through Glenashdale, with the burn on your right, past the fingerpost to the viewing platform for Glenashdale Falls: see page 64. Just beyond it, cross the burn by a footbridge and continue through the wood for 100 m or so, then turn right at a post through a gap in the stone wall.

Descend on a path through the sitka forest: within 200 m you reach an Iron Age fort on your right. You will see the exposed stones of its boundary wall, and the gap in the forest lets you appreciate its commanding situation.

After the fort, continue down across a footbridge with side-falls on the left, then through a boggy area with alder and ash. After a few steps up, look for the marker post pointing sharp left, uphill. (There's a viewpoint bench below, to the right.)

Within 100 m, emerge from the trees and meet a constructed path: turn left, uphill. The path soon meets the broad cycle track, where you turn right (north-east) for Lamlash. The forest road heads north, giving easy walking. The views are open at first – to the right South Ayrshire, with Holy Isle ahead – then closed off by trees.

After 1·5 miles (2·4 km) you reach Hawthorne Quarry. Climb the verge on the right to reach a picnic table with superb views across Whiting Bay to Holy Isle: see below.

Soon after, the track veers inland (north-west) and starts gently to descend. Clear felling has made gaps in the trees, and you pick up a stream to your left. The descent steepens, and the forest planting softens, with younger conifers and some birch, rowan and shrubs at its edge.

Exit the forest by a concrete bridge, through the gate and past the Dyemill car park (with picnic tables). The name derives from the former water mill, used in the textile industry. At The Ross (road), turn right and descend to the A841.

Turn left along the main road using the pavement wherever available. Over 300 m after crossing Benlister Burn, keep right to pick up the greensward beside Lamlash Bay.

East from Hawthorne Quarry

Lamlash to Brodick

Farm track approaching Clauchlands Point

On the left of the road, notice the Arran Clearances Memorial in front of the row of houses: see page 19. The Old Pier has a tea room, and the Holy Isle ferry leaves from here: see page 23.

- Keep to the shoreline of Lamlash Bay, but where the A841 veers left uphill for Brodick, instead go straight along the minor road. There's a long pavement stretch, with huge variety in the houses and gardens of the northern fringe of Lamlash.

- Signs explain the importance of this 'haul-out zone' for seals, and you may see them resting and drying out: please avoid disturbing them. Other signs explain the Lamlash Bay Marine Conservation Zone: Scotland's first No Take Zone that protects all species, whether they live in the sea or on the seabed. You pass the Outdoor Centre and your objective, Clauchlands Point, is clearly visible ahead.

- About 2 km after leaving the A841, the minor road turns left inland. Leave it here, keeping straight on through a timber pedestrian gate along a farm track (muddy in places).

- Within 1 km of the gate, you reach Clauchlands Point with Hamilton Rock to its east. Two World War II look-out shelters ('pill-boxes') are above, to your left. Keep to the shore, and after rounding the point, cross a fence by a stile.

Hamilton Rock, covered in sea birds

At this point, a narrow path on the left leads very steeply uphill to Dun Fionn fort. To stick to the main Way, skip to page 73. The case for the longer, more strenuous option is mainly the superb 360° view from the Iron Age fort (at 164 m/540 ft). Also, at an extreme high tide, you might wish to avoid the coastal marsh.

After climbing steeply, at first north-westerly, then west to reach the fort, the track descends with a right turn and continues north-westerly, eventually to pick up Corriegills Road after 600 m or so.

Follow the road for 1·2 km, then turn right for 400 m, finally turning left to rejoin the main Way (2·4 miles/3·8 km after leaving it) on a track heading down to Strathwhillan Road.

Steep path up to Dun Fionn

- To continue the main Way, ignore the Dun Fionn path, instead keeping ahead along the marshy coast, with views ahead to Goat Fell. The path narrows, passing through bracken, and after 2 km crosses a fence by a low timber stile. You are approaching a tiny settlement called The Dhunan, just short of Corriegills Point.

- At The Dhunan, turn left up the rough track to North Corriegills. The track heads generally west, climbing, then levels out and makes two doglegs on its approach to Strathwhillan Farm, passing over stiles. After a gap in the hedge and a right turn, you descend to the stile at the end of Strathwhillan Road.

- Turn left (west) along Strathwhillan Road for about 600 m to reach the A841. Turn right to descend to Brodick Pier within a further 400 m. If you want a souvenir, call in to the Douglas Hotel which issues a completion certificate and small badge (in 2017 for £2).

Timber stile on the approach to The Dhunan

Congratulations: you have completed the Arran Coastal Way. When you leave Brodick by ferry, aim to be on deck to take your farewell of Goat Fell, pictured below.

Reference

Management of the Arran Coastal Way

The Arran Coastal Way was devised by Dick Sim of Brodick, and first documented by the late Hugh McKerrell of Lochranza. The Way was opened in March 2003 by Cameron McNeish. The first Rucksack Reader was published in 2008 with sponsorship from five Arran businesses: Auchrannie Leisure, Bilslands, the Book & Card Centre, Isle of Arran Distillers and Best Western Kinloch Hotel.

Since 2012 the route has been managed by the Arran Access Trust. In 2014 -16 a project funded by the Coastal Communities Fund created many miles of new and upgraded path, with a variety of inland and coastal options. In 2017 the Arran Coastal Way was recognised as one of Scotland's Great Trails. We are grateful to Arran Access Trust and the Coastal Communities Fund for their generous support. To provide feedback on the route or waymarking, please contact *www.coastalway.co.uk*.

Contact details

Phone numbers are shown as dialled from within the UK. Numbers that begin 0871 attract a charge (often at 12p per minute).

Useful websites

The official Arran Coastal Way website is at
www.coastalway.co.uk
and it lists accommodation and other services. *VisitScotland* is Scotland's tourist board
www.visitscotland.com
There's a dedicated Arran destination website at *www.visitarran.com*
Wildlife websites include COAST (Community of Arran Seabed Trust), the annual Wildlife Festival and species such as red squirrel and basking shark are all linked from our page
www.rucsacs.com/links/acw.
Scottish Natural Heritage is the government agency that publishes SOAC and *Dog Owners* (see page 11): *www.snh.org.uk*

Notes for novices

Suggestions for novices on choosing and using gear are linked from our website home page: *www.rucsacs.com*.

VisitScotland iCentre

The island's visitor information centre is at Brodick Pier, open year-round. From April to September it is open 7 days a week until 17.00 (from 9.00, except10.00 on Sundays). Out of season it is closed on Sundays, but open 10.00-16.00 Mon-Sat. Tel 01770 303 774
brodick@visitscotland.com

Lochranza Youth Hostel

The Lochranza hostel (01770 830 631) is run by the SYHA and open April to October, booking recommended,. Membership is optional, and there's no upper age limit: in 2017 beds cost from £15 (shared rate), more for 2-4 person private rooms.
www.syha.org.uk

Emergencies

In an emergency, dial 999 and be ready to state the problem, location and number of people affected. The police will connect you to ambulance, Mountain Rescue or Coastguard as appropriate.

Service providers

At least 10 companies offer support services from baggage handling to complete self-guided packages for walkers. All are linked from our website
www.rucsacs.com/books/acw.

Tide tables

Tidal predictions are available from Admiralty EasyTide at
www.ukho.gov.uk/easytide/EasyTide/
They are provided free for up to one week ahead. Choose location either by clicking on the map or by searching for Brodick Bay, Lamlash or Loch Ranza. By default, times are shown in GMT: be aware that British Summer Time (GMT+1) applies from the last Saturday in March to the last Saturday in October.

Weather forecasts

Find BBC forecasts for Arran at
www.bbc.co.uk/weather or from the Met Office at *www.metoffice.gov.uk*. The latter finds results only for village names such as Brodick, Lochranza, Blackwaterfoot or Kildonan.

ARRAN
ACCESS TRUST

Public transport

Caledonian MacBrayne
   www.calmac.co.uk 08000 66 5000
for Arran, Kintyre and other ferries.
Buses to and within Arran are listed in a handy
Area Transport Guide booklet available on the
ferry or at the iCentre.

Traveline
For public transport within Scotland and the
UK, visit
   www.travelinescotland.com
   www.traveline.info
Or telephone 0871 200 22 33.
Scottish Citylink (Scottish buses)
   www.citylink.co.uk 0871 266 33

Airlines
British Airways *www.ba.com*
easyJet   *www.easyJet.com*
flybe   *www.flybe.com*
Ryanair   *www.ryanair.com*

Further reading

Collect a copy of the excellent *Arran Island Guide*
(free booklet published by *www.visitarran.com*)
from the ferry or iCentre.

Campbell, Thorbjørn (2013) *Arran: A History*
Birlinn 978-1-78027-110-1 Masterly overview
of human history from early settlers to modern
times, with poetry and folklore.

McLellan, Robert (2008) *Arran* (Pevensey Island
Guide) (David & Charles, 3rd ed) ISBN 978-
071532-891-0 Well-written and reliable, this
112-page book has been updated, this is a great
source on heritage, landscape, flora and fauna,
with many photos.

Kagyu Samye Ling Monastery (2007) *Holy
Island* ISBN 0-978-906-181-24-9 Explains the
island's history, Buddhist project and rare
breeds, with photos.

Online and printed maps

There's a detailed route map online at
   www.rucsacs.com/routemap/acw/ that
lets you zoom in for amazing detail. Use it for
planning or reminiscence.
Harvey Map's *Arran Superwalker XT25* map
shows the line of the route mostly correctly. In
2017 it cost £12.95 (waterproof):
   www.harveymaps.co.uk. The current (2015)
Ordnance Survey Explorer 361 does not yet
show the route: check before you choose.

Acknowledgements

The author thanks all those who helped with
her research trips and who commented on
drafts, especially Malcolm Whitmore,
Chairman of Arran Access Trust, who kindly
reviewed the whole manuscript. She thanks
also Stuart Blake for reviewing geology;
Scott Murdoch for his expertise on the
route and path works; Alex Roberts and
Neil McMaster for timely lifts; and Sandra
Bardwell for proofreading. She is deeply
grateful to Alastair and Alison Bilsland for
generous hospitality and practical support.

The multitude of comments received
resulted in many improvements, but we
accept responsibility for any flaws that
remain. We welcome feedback, preferably
by email to *info@rucsacs.com*.

Photo credits

Images are identified by page numbers with **u**
for upper, **m** *for middle and* **l** *for lower.*

Auchrannie Leisure Ltd 9u; Fiona Barltrop
15m, 49l, 52, 54-55; Ian Clydesdale title
page, 4-5, 6-7, 7 (upper 4), 9 (lower 3),
10l, 12, 13, 19, 24l, 25u & inset, 25m, 33u,
34 (inset 3), 36 (lower 2), 51u, 53, 54u,
72-73, back cover; Matt Edwards 25u;
Graham Chappell/Arran Graphics 34
(main), 45l; *Dreamstime.com/*Andreanita
28u; *Dreamstime.com/*Karen Appleyard
30l; *Dreamstime.com/*Fintastique 51l;
*Dreamstime.com/*Leo6001 30u; *Dreamstime.
com/*Lukas Blazek 26l; *Dreamstime.com/*
Mille 19, 40-41; Forest Life Picture Library
28l; Roger Griffith/Wikimedia Commons
29u; Jacquetta Megarry 6 (upper 4), 9
(lower 5), 11, 16u, 17u, 16-17, 22, 23, 24u,
24m , 25l, 32 (both), 35, 36 (upper 2), 38, 39,
41 (both), 43 (upper 2), 44 (both), 45u, 46
(both), 48 (all 3), 50 (both), 54m, 55 (both),
56 (both), 57 (all 3), 58 (both), 59, 60 (both),
61 (both), 62 (both), 64, 65 (both), 66 (all 3),
67, 68 (both), 70 (both), 71 (both), 72u, 73u;
Scott Murdoch 43l; Sir Gawain/Wikimedia
Commons p37l; Alex Pickup/*www.
iStockphoto.com* front cover; Chris Sharratt/
www.chrissharratt.co.uk 29l; Ben Slater/
www.iStockphoto.com 27u; Mark Townsend
18; VisitScotland 15.

Index